father

Zen

son

HACE

First published in 2009 by *Moyhill* Publishing.

Dutch language edition first published in 2007.
Original Dutch title: vader Zen zoon.

A CIP catalogue record for this book
is available from the British Library.

ISBN 978-1-905597-22-2

Translation by Tineke Zwartjes, Jim Webber and David Cronin.
Cover image painted by Hace.
Cover design and photos by Dolores Pallarés.

Printed in UK.

The papers used in this book were produced
in an environmental friendly way
from sustainable forests.

Moyhill Publishing,
Suite 471, 6 Slington House,
Rankine Rd., Basingstoke, RG24 8PH, UK.

Order online at *http://www.moyhill.com*

I am a part
of the whole
and the whole
takes part in me.

In every place
in every time,
at home
in my eternity.

Hace; It does.

Experiencing life during 24 hours camping together, as naturists, in 'the valley of the bridge' north of Tavascan.

A survival guide, beyond belief systems, towards self knowledge; with the possibility of staying alive during climate change.

Contents

Prologue

That morning, after the police car had brought his son home, long after midnight, the boy's question struck him unexpectedly.

"If someone can die suddenly, in the middle of a conversation, when he is only 18, then tell me, what is life about?" he had asked, looking defiantly at him.

In his clear blue eyes he could see that the devastation of that night had transformed into the rage which precedes grief or, sometimes, dismay.

The challenging way in which it was posed asked for more, much more, than just an answer – however well-meant.

It hadn't been difficult to sense that the question led to an inevitable conclusion. A compelling conclusion that had to be taken seriously, and had to be welcomed as being of crucial importance to his son's development. As a result, he had returned with the proposition that had brought them here, now. Here at the end of this green valley north of Tavascan.

Almost half a century of age between them disappeared as the extremely intimate form of nature surrounding them revealed itself to both of them.

They were truly in the lap of Mother Nature. Between impressively high-rising arches of rock, unimpeded, nature had created a soft, symmetrical oval enfolding a waterfall and a bubbling mountain stream. It was as if they were enclosed in Mother Nature's own generous, magical, life-giving genitalia.

Again he was astonished by the harmony; the spirit-healing energy of a bubbling mountain stream that manifested itself in the unforced and natural way in which the boy made him a part of his thoughts, feelings and questions. A communication that took shape within the intense feelings of oneness, of union and intimacy that he could now experience.

Now there was no separateness between them.

I   That morning

The bewildering death of his school-friend of many years had happened suddenly, while they were talking about their choice of subjects, student flats and their future expectations. It had been their first week at college and this death had made him feel completely disconnected from his own life – unable to have, or own, his future. Suddenly, and for the first time, he felt that the reality of a future, the future, his future, existed only in conversations about it. Talking about it had formed the foundation of his dreams and expectations of the future. And now he felt neither happy nor interested in his vision of himself and his recent choices for the direction of his studies.

*If he could die, now, just like that, what was the point in wasting the time that remained with what **others** thought necessary or useful for him? Why should he get involved in all kinds of theories about himself, and of some theoretical long-term future? Why should life **now** be postponed until later?*

He felt his interest in all the activities of the introduction week drop to zero and decided not to participate. Amazed, he realised that, as far as he was concerned, the study of economics could go to hell. He felt that it had been a choice based on not knowing anything better.

He felt anger rising: anger about the life that had taken away his best friend and thus his faith. Anger about feeling manipulated by all those well-meaning people around him. By their expectations of him; by their "truths" and convictions and the unspoken message: *"we have expectations that you need to measure up to, so don't disappoint us"*. He could only guess at what these expectations might be since he had been left the space to make his own choices.

But now he needed know how real these truths and convictions were. *On which facts or fantasies were they based? Was it really about the life of a human being, for whom each day could the last, regardless of age?*

He felt the anger subsiding and giving way to the sensation of being cheated. To have pretended that experience gained by others was more important than the life he had to experience – here, now, and in his own way.

He was astonished that he had so easily let himself believe that twelve years of going to school every day was not enough; that he should spend the next four to six years again in an artificially lit building – shutting everything out... sun, wind, rain, snow, his friends... and turning his back to occupy himself with the knowledge and thoughts of others. Second-hand knowledge for which the price would be his freedom and happiness. He realised in a flash of reluctance that this price was too high and he would not be paying it.

He would go and spend his time with his friends in situations that he could enjoy and from which he also could learn something every day; whatever. As soon as he reached this conclusion he realised that it was already a decision: A decision to do something that was not clear-cut and recognised. A decision for which he would certainly not be thanked.

He tried to imagine how his father would react. His decision might be respected but certainly not his motivation. He could see his father's analytical mind greeting his decision with a certain amount of irony as he shredded the logic behind it: He could already hear his father asking – out of interest, of course – "Do you honestly think that this new approach to life is really tenable? How useful are your friends really going to be, and what could you really expect to learn from tagging along with them?" Or even; "What is the sense of just enjoying life? Tell me more about all these situations you think to create. How do you see these? What am I supposed to think about that?"

He could see the conversation ending up with the inevitable question: "And you expect to earn your bread doing that?" Time and again that *bread*, as though life could only be worth living if directed solely by bread.

In an almost amusing flash of insight he thought, "How *useful* are flowers, actually?" But his heightened sense of insecurity didn't lessen in any way as the thought passed through his mind, on the contrary, it got stronger when his father walked in, and he found himself blurting out: *"If someone can die suddenly,*

*in the middle of a conversation, when he is only 18,
then tell me, what is life about?"*

It sounded a lot angrier than he had intended.

The gentle: "Good question! I will gladly get back
to you about it this evening", from the man walking
away, surprised him completely.

II   The valley

His father got back to it that evening and, for him, in an unusual way. Not clear and analytical. Not as sharp and thought through as usual. Why had he not looked forward to that evening, he wondered. *And... how well did he really know his father?*

"When I tell you that life is really about itself," his father said, "it won't make you much wiser and at best you might go away and think about it."

The first thing his father had said was surprising enough, and then the completely unexpected proposal to go to "his valley". To go to that place of his, together; "because there," he had said, "you will be able to experience How."

Carefully, he asked whether his father was very sure about wanting to share his secret retreat and was told: "It is not about sharing that place – it is... we are going... we are going to heal you."

Then, yet again, that amazing togetherness which he had already felt so strongly.

"We are going to let you experience and feel How life revolves around *itself*," the man next to him had said.

And now they sat here, together, beside this bubbling stream.

During the drive in, he hadn't particularly noticed the form of the valley. Then, on the bridge the comparison took his breath away. Mother Nature had absorbed them into her most intimate part. Enclosing them totally in her lap. Took them to herself. United herself with them.

Quietly, they had stayed on the bridge watching the waterfall's white, bubbling stream winding between all those green bushes. Towards the arching mountainsides that bowed towards each other like massive labia and crowned at their junction with a high, flat top as though it were the clitoris. There, above the watery crevice in this tender green oval, underneath sharp blue, he had, for the first time, experienced himself as part of the whole – and realised within himself that the whole was also a part of him.

At that moment his father had spoken:

"Life, the universal energy, is timeless; unchangeable. The life-forms, of which you and I are part, are permanently-changing carriers of that one eternal energy which has borne many names. Names for the un-nameable. Names that are thus not relevant; are of no importance; only give cause for confusion.

"What is relevant is that you understand, and feel, and can experience that this energy is made up of many frequencies. It is like a rainbow. It is constructed of frequencies in the same way that a rainbow is made of all colours.

"Each frequency also manifests itself in our world –

not as a colour, but in a specific, unique life form that pulsates. It appears; disappears; appears; disappears; and, when necessary, evolves. This means, by definition and in fact, that the process of appearing inevitably involves disappearing, and disappearing, appearing again. Always, everywhere, of everything and everyone, because energy doesn't get 'lost'. It can't 'disappear'. Where would it go?

"There is no need to weep when something or someone disappears since, for that very reason, it or they will always reappear. Our sadness and resistance against life – life as a permanent changing process that exists in an endless coming and going – is directed against the form. It is resistance against the pulsating of life forms because we don't understand their nature.

"The frequency that represents one universal, eternally unchanging life-energy is that content. Contents which seems to disappear when that form lets go, and blows life into another form; to manifest itself in another unique and similar life-form.

"It is like the fire on a hearth that continually forms different flames."

* * * * *

The concept had dazzled him – at first vaguely, then in its gigantic context: What remains of a rainbow if one pulls a colour or two out of it? Unimaginable!

And what of stones, trees, water, animals, air, everything of nature he could see here? *Demonstrating the same energy that expressed itself within him? Merely, solely, of different frequencies?* But that would mean that trees or water were worth exactly as much as he himself!

Suddenly he remembered a hilarious moment. It was at the science lesson:

"So, if I understand you correctly," his best friend had said to the teacher, "what happens during a walk in the woods is just the filling up of my lungs with the stinking exhalation of all those trees around me!"

"Yes. Without chlorophyll, without green matter, no animal life and therefore no human life," had been the dry answer, and with a shock he realised that only now did he understand that answer: The deforestation of our planet is like a macro lung cancer. And all those screaming chainsaws are cutting into our own lungs.

A cold sweat came over him. A feeling of unease, of danger, and the feeling that he was being physically attacked took control of him. *Was anyone **doing** anything about that? Who was looking after his interests? Did no one actually understand that it meant macro future suicide? Why did politicians only neutralise each other's actions, he thought, instead of banishing this kind of criminality?*

Why doesn't the leader of the new large 'Roman empire' now devote himself to the wellbeing, the life-breath of existing people instead of the life-breath of those who are yet to come or are almost no more?

Why does this autocrat not order his black-uniformed forces to mobilise his disciples, and world opinion, against what is happening, instead of letting himself and his 'bachelor' army merely celebrate Mass? For whose benefit? Pretending caring, yes even "holy" fatherhood. Preaching celibacy and a behaviour like stewards of the earth. Based upon what?

* * * * *

The questions tumbled over each other while he looked with disbelief at the man next to him. *How was it possible for him to stand there quietly, radiating peace?*

Surely all of this will have struck him as well, he thought. He had taken his father's hand to walk off the bridge to the place where they were now sitting. It was close to a wading pool, or maybe it was a drinking-place for cattle? He had seen a lot of horse droppings in several places, on the path and behind the big, coarse natural-stone wall alongside the path, but there hadn't been a horse in sight anywhere, and the birds, butterflies and lizards or chameleons, not at all shy, seemed to have this empire all to themselves.

Crystal-clear water in the calm parts of the shallow stream revealed, down to the pebbled bottom, a complete absence of fish. Yet signs, forbidding fishing without a permit, were an indication of bureaucracy and pursuit of gain. Over-fishing, just like that over-sawing, he had wondered. Were permits granted according to rules and the law? Or were they based on gain for someone's benefit?

In silence, side by side, they walked on. Over the winding, grass-covered, stony path that rose and disappeared between yellow flowers and the drooping tender green of the birches along the river's edge which had repeatedly given them glimpses of the bubbling stream. They seemed fragile, in strong contrast with the generously grey-bearded, mossy members of the same species at the other side of the path. The whole perfectly fitting in with the many fluttering, colourful butterflies approaching and then passing them by.

Just as surprisingly colourful and multi-shaped as the butterflies were the many large, moss-covered stones alongside the road. Extraordinarily well fitting, stacked in and on each other by human hands; rock lumps joined together as a whole. They seemed to belong there, to have always been there. Part of and in harmony with the whole, but in fact the result of centuries of stacking by many generations of toiling farmers reclaiming the land for their existence. Forming a cultural historical monument of priceless value. Something that deserved, out of respect, the upkeep by the present generation, he mused, while starting to take of his shoes.

If that land hadn't been reclaimed, made stone-free, the walls wouldn't have stood as tangible proof of co-operation by those generations – and neither would the present generation. Preserving that work by repairing damage from tree roots would honour the predecessors, from whom the land was inherited, to make possible a relatively easy existence. These thoughts passed through his mind.

Following his father's example, he too decided to take off his clothes and they walked together, naked, into the stream. Moving towards the rapids where the water dropped white and bubbling, in between big boulders.

The cool water felt velvety and, surprisingly, not

at all cold, and carefully, foot by foot, feeling the big pebbles on the bottom, he waded towards a big boulder in the middle. Fascinated, he watched the swirls immediately behind a grey-brown slice of rock, oblong and smooth as a mirror, rising to just underneath the surface. A bubbling, silvery, whirling, three-dimensional artwork playing with sunlight. The water surface behind took on the structure of the wrinkled skin on his grandmother's forearm. After a while he walked around it carefully, almost stumbling, on the way to the pebble-bed in the middle. The water seemed to be calf-deep and apparently flat with vaguely-visible, autumn-like colours.

Although the turbulence increased and the visibility decreased as he approached the rapids, the bottom remained visible through the clean water which was no more than knee-deep. Not until now, right in front of this one, he saw the sequence of shallow falls behind it – an unexpected long row of scattered, foaming ledges between large and small boulders.

He could not hear what his father shouted, above the splashing and roaring, but he could clearly see how he lay, stretched out in the narrow passage between rocks, letting himself be powerfully hydro-massaged. He needed no encouragement to follow the example. A good act to follow well, he thought while carefully choosing his own well-fitting Jacuzzi.

III   The river

Lying in the cool bubbling water, he enjoyed its freshness, at least 30 degrees cooler than the air, while the boy stood attentively watching the upper course of the water terraces beside him. The water was barely up to the knees of his tall body — he was more than two metres tall and as athletic as a Greek god, thanks to competitive swimming and more than five years of water-polo. What a splendid human being.

What a privilege to be here, now, for development of his son's emotional body. A whole gamut of divergent feelings came over him. How he had, during a time of trouble and tiredness, found this place. So long ago. It felt as if it had been only yesterday, or more like last week — and yet still wonderful, even though it had been more than 30 years ago.

He also felt the familiar satisfaction at having successfully kept this place private. During all those years of ignoring questions and requests about it. Demanding at times the right be alone;. to be with himself, without always having others present. Not to have to listen to voices. Not even his own voice or to those of others. Or to the voices from electronic gadgets.

To be able to concentrate exclusively on listening to the 'the voice' of his own heart.

The thankfulness, at this place, at some moment, to be able to experience that voice within the sound of birds, wind, water. Without any exertion to suddenly know what he really needed now. Again and again, always again; suddenly that crystal clear knowledge. *That*; that's it. That is what I have to do now. No matter how preposterous it had seemed. He had never tried to barter or trade with it. Despite all the consequences.

With amazement he had always noticed that, straight after such moments of clarity, his analytical brain would have already become occupied with the "*How*" question. How then to create and realise that, in a practical, sensible way. Fairly quickly, he also realised that his mind hadn't been equipped to answer the "*What*" question. Nor did he know the mind of others, he discovered later when evaluating the results in the form of judgements, philosophies, doctrines and dogmas…. artificial and perhaps fantasies.

Again he felt gratitude and amazement for the moment where he could become aware of this. The moment in which he understood that 'the whole' had let him know, again and again, what he really needed. Let him know what it was that he really needed for continued growth of self-insight and for his further development. Insight also into the world around him. The insight, of being in touch with the earth, the air, the water, the sun's warmth, the light softness of the moon, between the sparkling stars, forming a compass which guided him and held him in balance. Protected him from getting lost in the fantasy world of beliefs, hopes, ideology and economy. Prevented him from losing grip on the reality of one's own experience, one's own integrity. Now, again, he was astonished at the completely individual and unusual manner in which he had created, socially and economically, a suitable place without having had to sell his body and soul. The effortlessness with which it had presented itself – in a sort of organic process of growth; the one coming forth out of the other.

"Do you never need to make an effort for anything?" it had been said, half-jokingly or a bit jealously.

"Ah, why would I choose effort by resisting who or what presents itself?" he had lightly replied. "I'd rather welcome who and what presents itself. To make the best of that and just trust it – that will be enough."

Usually, after this response, the conversation would come to an end. He had created a single rationale from his grandmother's intriguing statement: "*Whoever doesn't search for his ease is lazy*". That effectively closed the discussion.

Yes, he himself, becoming aware of wholeness through unity, had been protected from leading a specific career; it had enabled him to lead a less defined life. He had been able to change roles more than once in the economics of life. Taking all the so-called risks and discomforts into the bargain and enjoying a new occupation, gathering the necessary knowledge, using his natural curiosity to make himself familiar with the needed knowledge and skills. Instead of joylessly repeating himself to obtain results, he continued to experience the enjoyment of accomplishment by doing just that. *"As one welds, one becomes a blacksmith"*. He had remembered this whenever things were more difficult than expected – and not only in France, the country of origin of this proverb, but also here-and-now.

He looked at the water gushing over the boy's shoulders, gathering around the solid neck under the blond curls.

"What then is life about?" he thought, and felt he was getting peckish. "Are you coming to eat?" he shouted in the direction of the back of the boy's head while he slowly stood up. On the bank he found the shoulder bag and took out the thermos flask, to fill its big lid with green tea.

"Life is about bread, but more about love," he mused, looking at the two French loaves, the wine and olive-oil bottles near the chunk of goat's cheese at the bottom of the bag. After all *without* her love for her lover, his older friend, the boy would not be here. Nor, for that matter, without his own love he realised, thinking back 19 years to that decision, taken in the knowledge that each man may be the father of all children. Taken, too, from his own painful experience of having grown up fatherless.

Who are my mother and father? Are they not the people who consciously demonstrate and pass on what makes life worth living for them? And also let themselves be questioned about this, to take responsibility, to give relevant answers instead of stock ones from institutions?

Thoughtfully, he looked at the boy, who was busy

drying himself, and suggested to him that they might go to the warm stones; the large basalt blocks polished smooth by centuries, maybe millennia, of streaming masses of water. One of his favourite spots, a natural heat-store that he went to after swimming to warm up. It seemed to him the ideal place for lunch.

* * * * *

He carried a bundle of clothes wrapped in a towel tucked under each arm, and the boy carried the bag of food, while they walked up to the old way out which was a few metres higher up the path, on the bank.

The abundance of little yellow flowers in the grass alongside the path brought him back to the banks of the lake of his youth. It was almost as good — still tangible, but the sunny days of Whitsun were already long gone. They were days when he, after a long winter without going on the water, canoed past green banks where he could climb onto the polder, the reclaimed land, when the reeds left enough room. The meadows behind the dikes would be mown late and revealed a multi-coloured palette of spring flowers. Could it be their smell which kindled his recollection?

He stepped carefully over the battery-fed electric fence (clearly meant to keep the horses inside) that separated the path from the meadowland that lay between the river and the two enclosed terraces.

While looking at the erosion debris of the steeply rising mountainside he walked further over the high part of the meadow and alongside the stream to where there was evidence of ore that looked a lot like an enormous piece of rusty scrap. He remembered again how once, squatting down, he had barely been able to accept that this would not turn out to be iron or metal. The seamless transition to the rocklike exterior of the plateau, a metre higher up, provided irrefutable evidence.

At the transition from rock to basalt, in the land running down to the stream, he realised he was standing on congealed earth-excrement, dating from the time mother earth still suffered from diarrhoea — which had been extremely liquid. Here, streamed from her intimate parts not cool, clear water but hot molten metal and stones at around 2,000 degrees Celsius. He realised he was in an ancient crater, standing on stones as old as the earth itself. At that instant he also understood why he had thought so strongly about the validity of a meteorite striking, when he had seen for the first time the sensational form of the valley.

Of course it *was* a crater. But from an eruption, not an impact. *Why* do we always, almost automatically, think about bringing inwards all that is on the outside? Instead of bringing out all that is within? These thoughts had formed the start of his awareness process. At once he had understood the concept of not just being on, and from, the earth but *just as much being **like** the earth*. Able to grasp the factual *reality*, needing only to propel it to birth. Nothing else. Just that? Already being capable of understanding everything, possessing the capacity, unable to take anything from outside to the inside other than *illusions* and fantasy. To be able to trust one's own knowing and perfection.

Being allowed to presume that the only "imperfection"

is this false judgement of himself (talked into him over the years), of being imperfect.

* * * * *

Suddenly, understanding came to him that, for the rest of his life, he would return again and again to this place of 'teaching by illustration'. To be able to recollect everything, here, which ought to be revealed. Here he would become conscious about 'forgotten' knowledge. Growing aware of his forgetfulness, and remembering that flawless awareness without wrongs or rationalisation, would give shape to his daily life.

Aware that his existence, his coming into being, here, concerned a *continuation* just as much as did the emergence of the mineral on which he stood. Everything, everyone, forming a continuation, an emergence of something that had already existed.

* * * * *

In a flash he had become the three or four-year-old boy again, confronted for the first time with an 'our father in heaven' who would 'give us this day our daily bread' and ought to forgive us something indistinct as well. He had heard this from the father of a friend, before they started to eat, one time when he was invited to share their meal. His clear insight during this experience was of being connected with the air, earth, water, sun and moon, and not at all with an 'our father'. Knowing that it was the baker who came by every week and who would actually deliver the large loaves of bread, if his mother gave him most of the eggs she gathered.

"He helps us with bread and we help him with eggs. That is more enjoyable than eating only bread or only eggs," is how she answered his question, "we exist here in order to help each other." About 'our father' who ought to have something to give, she had said nothing.

The result was that he was completely surprised, when, in that country kitchen, the devoutly praying farmhand had, for the first time, brought him in touch with the fantasy world that later would be called civilisation – civilisation that had caused his duality. For the first time he had been convinced of something he himself had not, could not and also would not experience, but on which his existence would depend?

"Believing in serving 'our Lord' makes it easier for the Lords to make us believe they need to be served," his mother had said to him, years later, "but with that *we* are not well served." And she added the warning "*never forget that*".

He had forgotten until that moment, but then it had remained with him vividly. It had even prevented him from letting himself be 'served' like a 'Lord' later on. In the service of profit creating workers who (as unavoidable costs) ought to be paid as little as possible. This in order to maximise his profit share after re-investing in *his* company and thus *also* in himself. He had passed up his turn to get into that fantastic system *of all for-one-and-one-for-none*.

He had chosen to provide himself with only an existence, an income, through helping others. Help came by saving time and/or money; through following other procedures and by making use of other resources. Trusting he would be granted the agreed part of the savings as reward for services rendered. Against others' expectations and cynicism he had never wanted either for bread or for eggs.

Still, his hen that had 'laid the golden eggs' was an ordinary farm animal and nothing special or spectacular.

"*Make something different from that which already exists, that which is already there, or change something that already exists into something different.*" The first he had, now and again, done. The second, now and again, not. His trust that he would be granted his share had never been betrayed – although occasionally it had looked like it might be. Choosing the un-trodden path instead of imitating and taking the beaten path with so many others, had brought him to a unique position. A position that he, moreover, did not need to defend with tooth and nail. He didn't have to maintain this position, through exploitation. Above all, it enabled him to express his creativity. Taking pleasure from creating – right up to the point of satisfaction in a completed creation. Again and again experiencing money as a result, a natural result of a healthy process, instead of a chancy goal.

"It is magical realism; the true reality," he had often thought. All fear of shortage is based on fantasy. The fantasy of separation and isolation. That fact had become clear to him through all those years.

* * * * *

And now he was sitting here with his son. Their bare buttocks comfortably seated in well-fitting dimples in nature's antique artwork. As a creation from a well-known artist it would immediately raise the prestige of a museum.

"It looks somehow like onyx" the boy had said, and then, in the same breath, asked if he also wanted olive oil first on his French bread. And then, before he was prepared for it, he continued with *"but aren't you scared, dad?"*

"No" he had answered. "I chose for happiness, happiness that I am alive. My life is my reality. A reality to celebrate, not to fear."

"But if it goes amiss, if something goes wrong with a couple of those 'frequencies' you were talking about, what happens to us then? Things aren't looking good for the ozone, trees, oil, fresh water and the air, and therefore surely also not for the 'person frequency'? Who can do something about that? Who can really take responsibility for it?"

The boy had looked at him penetratingly – and then proceeded to choke as he took a too-large mouthful of cheese with a swallow of wine.

Giving these questions, these serious questions, time to penetrate, he answered after a while: "I understand that this alarms you. That one universal, eternal, unchangeable life energy is a composition of frequencies, in which one seems able to manipulate one or the other without affecting the total.

"However, wherever or whenever that balance is disturbed it will be restored, with or without *our* exertion, with us as witnesses or without,. As long as we keep losing ourselves in fantasies about wanting to own, wanting to have the land, waters, the airspace and fire, so long shall we lose our right to exist.

"The earth brings *us* forth: *we* do not bring forth the earth. She possesses us and not us the earth. Your bare buttocks own this rock, who is your owner, you could say? Look at it in that way, the realistic way, and you will burst out laughing at the thought of someone saying to you that this, a million-year-old crater, is *his* property. How long and in what way has he been here? How long does he intend to stay here to look after his 'property'?"

"Also, there is another remarkable point and that relates to what one means by '*going wrong*'. But first something else:"

"All people have the earth and we can't *not* have it. The earth has all people but it *can* do without them. In fact, the earth might be better off if two thirds of them were not here − it needs overpopulation as much as you or I would need a toothache!"

"Unfortunately, the huge number of, so called, civilised people has already had an effect on the 'people frequency' and they have also had an enormous effect on the 'material' frequencies as a result of all the technological gadgetry that mankind has deployed. These affect the electromagnetic spectrum from the low frequency radio waves right up to the high frequency gamma radiation produced by radioactive substances.

"It is remarkable too that, in the fantasy world of civilisation, material possession, no matter the extent of that 'wealth', is experienced as insufficient. And this attitude of wanting to *own*, instead of to *use*, also extends to the non-material."

Mankind has invented many names, over the years, to try and describe the universal life-energy. Then, by monopolising their invented gods, their fantasies, these became the nucleation centres for conflict. This also precipitated the generation of all kinds of superficial thought constructions, with each brain-child, handed down from generation to generation labelled as being precious for maintaining their group identity.

The result of this is that no real responsibility is being taken for one's own life and one's own experiences in it, nor for one's own choices in reacting to those experiences and the feeling that stem from them.

Another result is that '*Listening to what one's own heart says*' has been placed in a bad light: disposed of and disregarded as 'manic' – after the enlightened Mani, who was also disposed of because he and his followers worldwide trusted their own experience of '*feeling*' the universal life-energy in the heart, and lived peacefully guided by that manifestation.

"Around 1,200 years ago, and once again about 800 years ago, the practitioners of this anti-authoritarian way of life were eliminated and 'the problem' settled in a 'christian manner'. The fantasy world of civilisation has, partially because of that, now reached a level of adoption where it is considered the accepted norm. As a result, the knowledge that emerges from life-experience, however realistic and real it becomes, is denied or discredited as being 'not scientific'."

"The question of one's own responsibility is thus passed over to the scientists, or other specialists. Or simply, coolly taken away with the help of all sorts of rules and regulations, which are forcefully imposed because they have been decided upon 'democratically' or even spoken ex cathedra, with the authority of the pulpit."

"In a certain sense the human-being 'frequency' has already gone wrong. The waste of minerals, greenery or water is not the *cause* of this but the *result*. A result of our own indulgence, fatuousness, ignorance. The missing quality is self-assurance and self-knowledge and therefore one's own personal responsibility and judgement."

"*Who can do something about it?* Everybody can do something about it. Everyone! Nobody, absolutely nobody is an exception. Everyone, in their own way, within their own limitations and opportunities can do something on one's own personal scale. Who takes the responsibility for that? *I, myself*, nobody else!"

At long last, he took a bite from the bread that had been passed to him, with a swallow of the Mestre Fruiters, the fragrant local wine. Silently the boy had been sitting, looking across the stream. There, on the black basalt, two snakes were moving slowly towards a split in the rocks. He was chewing at the same time and carelessly playing with the half-litre bottle of olive oil. He remained quiet for a long time.

Then, with mouth still half-full, he asked: "You mean me, don't you, surely? I, myself, nobody else?"

The answer came: "Precisely. Also you."

IV   The meadow

Although the snakes weren't poisonous, he nevertheless avoided the white, bubbling part of the waterfall to avoid an unseen encounter with these eel-like swimmers. In the clear water a bit further along, it was more than a meter and a half deep, the swimming had been good. In the sun, out of the wind, the temperature had gone over 50 degrees C.

It was something he had never experienced in all those years, at that time of the year. The boy however, unable to make the comparison, welcomed the warmth for what it was with a joyful spluttering and splashing of which he could not get enough. Even so, couple of times he had the impression he was going to be approached. In the water it hadn't happened. Nor later on, during the drying-time on the stones, with the feet still ankle-deep in the water.

Quickly he suggested they go to the meadow, his beloved place of meditation. Higher up and seemingly central, between the high rock walls that receded on both sides, there was always some wind. And further along behind the trees the sharp-blue sky seemed to disappear as in a funnel. Enjoying the warm wind's caress along his naked body he had spread out his towel among the buttercups and scant grass. He was impressed again by the soft, clean energy at this place with many whirling butterflies in irregular flight. It was inconceivable that an infernal sea of fire had once dumped poisonous debris here, he mused.

Until that question came: *"How then to do that, to take responsibility on one's own personal scale? How could that be enough?"*

The boy had posed the question while lying stretched-out, leaning on one elbow, chewing on a blade of grass. But what had the boy really intended, he wondered, with this seemingly rhetorical question?

For a moment he had hesitated but then decided to take one more swallow of wine before saying: "The *How* takes care of itself when *you* take care of the surrounding factors, the essential preconditions."

A large orange butterfly had come and fluttered around him, though without distracting him from this important and practical question. And he continued:

"Those factors mean taking care of the right circumstances. They have to be right, and absolutely necessary, to enable what has to take place to happen. To be able to let itself develop. Then you, or I, or whoever provides takes the action, becomes aware of the *How* of his own accord. Without having to alter anything more. Self-insight arises – the possibilities and restrictions of oneself and the ability to apply them – by acting, using them. And this requires a decision of will. A possibility, after all, implies that a conscious choice has to be made."

He saw in the boy's eyes that he had not been able to follow easily. That he had probably never experienced such a high level of abstraction. He realised he would have to be more pictorial and that he would have to shed some light on the difference between starting points and essential preconditions.

Thus he had not gone further into the question of decisions of will. The courage for that had to be found necessary – the courage coming from trust in acquired insight. Often, very often contrary to prevailing ideas, it was a matter of appraising the opinion of others with the only defence a reference to "common sense".

* * * * *

"Starting points are fixed – they can't be held up for question or discussion," he had stated. "In this case, taking personal responsibility in daily life is taken as the starting point and is therefore unshakeable. Neither by others nor by yourself. But the surrounding factors are changeable, and they determine to a large extent the growth of awareness – in the same way that earth, light, water and warmth are needed for a seed to grow to a plant. One can't *make* a plant. A seed does that by itself. It lets itself develop when the surrounding conditions are suitable. And if the right conditions and circumstances continue, the result of that process is a plant. Likewise, one cannot undergo an awareness process. Under some conditions it can become complete in you and result in insight. Acquired insight. More self-knowledge."

"Thus, certain circumstances are changeable and

these will be different for each person, and also different at different stages of life. However, there are other, common factors that apply to everybody, and at any stage of life, and those surrounding conditions are of crucial importance for progress and the pace of the awareness process."

The blade of grass had been removed from the mouth, signifying that he had all of the boy's attention. The involuntary movement, like using a baton, had encouraged him to come out with it now.

Putting on his straw hat he started with the most challenging of all:

– "Each time one knows something intuitively, that knowing can be superseded by rationalisation. Never ignoring and always taking seriously something vague and un-provable – unfounded information – is difficult to justify to others. Then don't justify it. Just act on it. Always take intuition as seriously as the mind – they are complementary parts. This is number one in the surrounding factors."

– Each time that your mind boggles when something is not as it should be, with conclusions or proposed measures from politicians, clergy, technologists, academics from any discipline or organisation whatsoever, it is essential to keep a sharp eye on your final responsibility for your own wellbeing in your own life – and if necessary act within your means. Always take common sense just as seriously as the so-called expertise of specialists. You have a more general view and that means complementary. This is surrounding factor number two.

– Each time that your intuition lets you know what to do or what not to do, think specifically of '*how*' and not '*if*', to give it form. Intuition as a compass, common sense; the intellect as a roadmap to be completed with the courage of actually taking that road instead of fantasizing about it. This is surrounding factor number three.

– To actually follow your road each time is your personal creation that adds something to the whole, because you are a part of that. That is enough. If you follow that path you are being complementary, and that makes every fantasised 'goal' superfluous. That is surrounding factor number four.

– Each phenomenon or manifestation turns, sooner or later, to the opposite as each reality is built up out of pairs of opposites. One side presents itself in the first instance and the other half of the pair manifests itself later. Both halves, however present themselves without providing a view of the whole that represents *all* facts – in the same way that neither day *nor* night show their *whole* twenty-four-hour cycle.

So welcome everything. Don't pass *judgement* on anything or anyone. Whatever something or someone seems, it is always only the immediately visible part. The opposite exists and will, at some point, become apparent as well. Although, how long or short a time it may take to do so is unknown.

Searching, finding and staying in balance by avoiding

being judgemental is the fifth, most important and most difficult to realise, surrounding factor in one's own awareness process, and the one which can lead to true self-knowledge."

* * * * *

After that and for all that, he nevertheless also pointed out other variable factors. Like work and surroundings, study, relationships, ambitions. The fact that definitely shaped work and living conditions can be changed easily but relationships and ambitions not so easily. He pointed out the aging resistance of the immaterial aspects in personal relationships, compared with the 'limited shelf-life' of relationships with material objects in life. Because of this he had himself mostly experienced the substantial, rather than the insubstantial, as abstract. He had explained that taking one's own responsibility for the whole, on one's own personal scale, would indeed be 'enough is enough'. He explained how this happens and *How* to give that shape in daily life. He also gave the example of a damaged hologram, pointing out that the three-dimensional image information imprinted on the complete photo-plate was reflected in each piece of the broken glass, no matter how small the piece. He explained that in all the pieces of such an image the whole was made visible through each fragment being part of that whole. This would also imply that if there was a change in one of the broken pieces then this change would be reflected in all of the pieces, and in the whole of the image.

"Is that, then, the deeper meaning of 'change the world, then start to change yourself'?" the boy had asked – much to his surprise – showing he had understood it completely. "But then," he exclaimed, "I don't have to be my brother's keeper at all. Then I don't have to prove myself right. No need to dispute the opinions, beliefs and behaviour of others. Developing my own beneficial exemplary behaviour for myself and the people around me should be enough."

"Leading yourself to effective beneficial behaviour will certainly ensure followers. Just like the example of the hologram; when the image in one small bit changes... like that, the image which they exhibit will have to change when the image which you display, changes," he had affirmed. The change of a part of the whole implies that the whole will become, different,

"Understanding how to lead yourself to effective, salutary behaviour is not so easy, because it isn't taught at schools or universities – nor in society. Sooner discouraged than stimulated," he had said, "because the rendering of services through institutions and systems is first-of-all aimed at the continued existence and well-being of those very organisations and systems. This is implicitly considered to be of greater importance than the welfare of the people for whom they exist."

Even the worldwide organisation that forms the powerful carrier of the Christian belief system, surprisingly enough, does not form an exception to this phenomenon.

Out of the thermos flask came yet another big mug-full of green tea. He realised they were tremendously fortunate with this unusually beautiful weather, which made it possible to spend the night under the open sky, instead of in his beloved and excellent hotel *Llac de Cardos.* A sky which undoubtedly would stay deep blue. Through which all the stars, including the Milky Way, would become visible once the sun had set.

He remembered his own, and the boy's, child-like fear of the dark. He wondered if by now the boy had outgrown his need of a night-lamp. In any case, the moon would make a lantern unnecessary. A woollen blanket over the sleeping bags would provide enough protection against the dew that he knew from experience would come just before daybreak.

While he took hold of the empty mug handed to him by the boy, the question came that he had been long expecting. It was also, at this moment, very logical:

"Why then go to university; how really necessary is that?"

"It isn't so much necessary as practical," he had answered. And left it at that for the time being, with the promise to get back to it later. And then proceeded to explain that direct investment of time and energy in the immaterial, like in a fine education, is very profitable, in every aspect. This, in contrast with investing time and energy in material aspects of life at a young age. Also that, as a life's aim, collecting material possessions means missing the essence of life. This, because material existence and material realisation only are natural consequences of having chosen a direction of positive intention and input on behalf of the whole. The magnetic field of this attitude, this life mentality, attracts what is essential in a way for us to be able to exist. It manifests itself in the form of support through the whole, in both material and immaterial senses.

With that he had answered the most important part of the *'How to give that shape in daily life'* question – although not yet specifically.

The boy commented that taking responsibility for one's own life didn't have to mean a fight at all. No competition and no confrontations emerging from those annoying little incidents that he had always expected until this time. According to his feelings now, it meant a process of continuous co-operation.

"Exactly," he said. "For me and you. It is important as well to accept yourself completely *as you are*. Including your so-called *'bad'* qualities – the *'dark'* side. By doing so, you will be able to avoid the illusion of being different – and better than others. With that attitude it becomes self-evident that you respect others entirely as being different. And that you leave behind the idea of passing judgement on yourself and on others.

Remember that a judgement is only a subjective *interpretation* of facts, and then seeing this interpretation is an important fact in itself. However, it is *not* a fact and may never become that. Because that could lead to the kind of behaviour through which wars have been unleashed. And this does not relate exclusively to the past. Even quite recently this kind of devastating disaster has taken place.

"Judging and passing judgement comes from an unconscious *negative* intention and input, which is meant for 'the benefit' of the whole."

He had warned against aggression, or getting into fights, under whatever beautiful name it was known and for whatever goal it was meant to achieve. Aggression always takes place on the basis of judging and passing judgement. He had explained also that 'peace army' that kills can exist only through mislead ignorance. Such armies are send and sponsored by people who have been provoked in some way and who do not realise that '*vinegar simply stays vinegar even if a chateau wine-label is stuck on the bottle;*' by democratically-chosen demagogues selling violence. Enticers who are obsessed by their own alleged interest.

In any event, the 'magnetic field' of this negative attitude inevitably attracts loss, and causes material and potential (immaterial) loss. However, in personal life that is not always directly apparent, because input and result take place in different places and times. Because of this, the results become rationalised in public life, and played down or neglected in silence through opportunism as well.

"If all of us were instantly confronted, here and now, with the consequences of our thoughts, feelings, utterances and action, the law of cause and effect (consequences) would inspire us with awe and respect. This law, which is as inexorable as it is invisible, would then receive our *full* attention and be painstakingly respected – instead of being neglected, set aside and played down with remarks like "but that's a coincidence"; "how lucky"; "what bad luck"; "why did I deserve this" and "if God existed then how could he allow this to happen?; and so on."

"It is significant to hear people quote "*as ye sow, so shall ye reap*" and "*who gives what he has is worthy of life*". Moreover, in the christian bible, it is said that "*he who lives by the sword shall die by the sword*". Both theories are in fact correct."

He had resolved his argument and a silence fell in which only the river could be heard.

V   The reality

One thing is clear, he had thought, after his father's argument, and that is that nothing appears to be what it seems to be. At the most, at the utmost, perhaps half of it – and that not exclusively. With increasing amazement he had seen a reality appearing in, or behind that which was apparent. At a certain moment, he realised with some bewilderment that this man wasn't just capable of answering questions but *lived* those answers himself, daily. And in such a way that he was now presented with the *How* and *What* – the essence of which had never really got through to him.

Yes, his father was an unusual man, certainly, with his own style and approach and with very much his own ideas, too. But he didn't know any different. His father had not surprised him often, but his friend's fathers had. And he had sometimes had the impression that they wanted to be funny when, on the contrary, they were very seriously philosophizing or orating. They had rarely been grateful when he had approached it jokingly. Must be my unusual sense of humour, he had thought then. Slowly he had been getting used to the idea that he would never be appreciated if he took things in a humorous way. Moreover, he had become vaguely aware that he had never really found them to be funny or truly interesting anyway. He had been more than once surprised by the judgemental arguments about others – never focusing on themselves. Always about the thoughts, feelings and actions of others instead of sharing, their own experiences and feelings. Surprised, he wondered how it was possible that this man, with each question he answered, seemed to raise more questions. Even although those answers were sometimes shocking, they were to-the-point and unambiguous.

How was it possible that this man turned out to be so different than he had seemed to be for the last 15 years. But he bore with this, behind all that knowledge of the specialist and expert who, as an appreciated and respected member of the community, played his role relaxed and sure in the economy. The 'game' that he said to experience as a fantasy world in which the false, fashionable conviction is the need to survive at the expense of others. A conviction that was diametrically opposed to his and which would probably make daily life extremely stressful. Strangely enough however, it accomplished the opposite, and delivered evidence of the value of reality. Making visible the reality behind or in the '*reality*'; that reality of which he had spoken in terms of energy and attitude.

In the long silence, he reflected on the consequences of war and peace, competition and co-operation, positive attitude and input, or negative. He had understood why the law of cause-and-effect had not been dealt with in science lessons. Despite this, he knew that it absolutely *did* belong there as well: next to the law of the gravity and the law describing the upward power of a 'body' partially or completely immersed in a liquid. This omission wasn't caused through lack of interest in this law, he now understood, but through the impossibility of capturing it in words and recording it adequately. Maybe the omission also arose from applying it in behavioural terms, and thus causing difficulty in measuring its application; and through the distance in time and place that appear between cause-and-effect, and an inability to get a perspective on this.

He then recognised the resulting *interference* that occurs between collective and individual causes-and-effects. This unavoidable disturbance leads to confusion which, in turn, produces 'natural pollution'; as a camouflage of individual actions in relation to the consequence of those actions.

In any case, he himself felt convinced of the existence of this law; of the reality of this law behind 'accidental' or arbitrary happenings in the 'reality'. The image of the law of gravity and the holidaying mountain climbers he had seen hanging against a steep rock face forced itself powerfully upon him. If one should lose one of the climbers – connected to the rest of the group and willing to be part of the group's care – that one would fall as a consequence of the law of gravity, but not disastrously. On the other hand, in the event of *not* being a part of the group, and wanting to go 'solo' and achieve just for his own benefit, he would at first climb more quickly, and probably with less effort, by not having to take others into consideration. But during a long, complicated climb he could become increasingly exposed and in the event of a fall could be severely injured.

In the end, within that group of five or six, one would reach the top by one's own strength. But even if all should do that, except for one or two, would there be happiness about the achieved performance and also the incredible view? Or only sadness?

"So, choosing to connect to the whole is choosing for yourself and choosing life? Choosing to withdraw from the whole, the illusion of isolation is the same as refusing food – in fact, starvation," he had said quietly.

At that point he had stood up to go for a walk, leaving his father behind in the meadow with the bag and the towels. Naked, he had, under the white cap, walked to the bridge after remarking on the need to let this dawn on him. At the bridge, in the shade, stood a red jeep. This suggested the presence of someone who apparently didn't believe in an empty river and now, in all probability, with the aid of one of the fishing rods from the jeep, was trying to outwit a trout. It was nice that he could stand here for his pleasure. Not like a hundred or maybe only 50 years ago because he had to eat, he had thought.

Above the white bubbling water, green-bordered on both sides, he had gone to hang on the middle of the bridge over the parapet. Looking between the green slopes at a large snow patch below the obtuse angle of the mountain-top, straight in front of him.

"Still sperm on clitoris-hill," he muttered, "and it's

already June. No wonder that so much water flows here." Immediately after that he formed in his mind's eye a vision of life and death as one whole. As different stages of the same. Or, how had his father put it, again? Oh, yes, as complementary. Both components of one, eternal, unchangeable, universal life-energy. Pulsating and manifesting themselves in different frequencies through appearing in different life-forms and proceeding by disappearing out of those again.

That my being here, no my Being, thus represents the temporary as well as the eternal. Hey, that is funny, flashed through his mind: That the present time is part of the eternal is logical. And just as logical that eternity is by that also part of the present time. And thus represents itself in that. How illogical that I have never seen that myself. I haven't been able to see that for myself. Myself as eternal, in the present time. Exactly as much for contents as for form. As much material as immaterial. The synthesis!

"But why do I get this sudden image of life and death, now?" he asked himself silently, looking at sunlight reflecting on the birch leaves of an overhanging branch right in front of the bridge. Ah yes, that blob of sperm; that slab of grimy white snow, the bubbling stream, ice, water, river, ocean, evaporation, fog. Rain, snow, ice... No start, no end of life through birth and death. They are transitions from the one invisible dimension, via the visible for us to the other, or who knows, same invisible dimension. The water that reaches the sea or ocean as river does not cease to exist even though it does, as river, become invisible. Nor does the snow that disappears and reappears as water. They are transformations, a change from one transformation phase, or physical appearance, to the other.

Pupating caterpillars die? Yes, they are 'dying' to rise up and fly out as butterflies. *But how dead is that caterpillar?* Even although this little animal no longer crawls around anymore over the earth. *Is human death a pupation?* What was the essence of his no-longer-living 18-year-old friend, through whose shocking, sudden death he was now here? *What did his father want, between the lines, to make really clear to him?*

* * * * *

"When we step out of the fantasy-world of fears, hopes and expectations, forgetting all those well-meant bedtime fairy tales, and confine ourselves to *The* reality of facts, then there is no discord. No I–vs–you but exclusively *one united creation*: *We.* And that counts for everything; always," he had said just before they drove into the valley.

Would that mean…? Disconnection through distance and difference of frequency is a false reality? By the grace of the physical restrictions; that was obvious.

But is the disconnection through time and transformation phase different?

That too. His mind stood still. After a little while, or it might have been a long time, he noticed that his mouth was agape. He felt goose bumps not only on his arms but also on his neck and legs. He vaguely began to understand how his father possessed that calm but also the unbelievably immense creative power. That man truly understands all this and he never confronts

– anybody. Indeed, no reason for sadness about his friend. Yes, about missing their conversations. And not being able to laugh together anymore. *But was his sadness now caused by a fact or a thought? Had his friend evaporated, or only his body?*

Suddenly he remembered the holiday that they weren't able to take; not able to go camping on the moors together because he had been told enthusiastically that he (his friend) was going to Canada with the whole family that summer. Uncles who had emigrated long ago had repeated their invitation for the umpteenth time, and now insisted that the family cross the ocean. Had he been sad at hearing this decision? Not exactly. Not even disappointed about the month-long absence during that trip to Canada. He had realised that already they had camped so long, so often together that this new experience for him ought to be welcome. And not only by his friend. By him, the one who stayed behind, as well. He had trusted that some other companion for that holiday on the moors would announce himself. And in a way it had indeed happened. During that holiday his absent friend had appeared strangely present. In spite of being out of reach his name came up often. He was even toasted at meal times. Thus also now he had just gone somewhere else, he saw. The only difference was that he stayed away longer, stayed 'there'.

What does it actually matter that I am still locked up in my physical transformation phase, while he is already again in the non-material phase?

Because of that I am unable to observe with my senses his now shapeless, body-less existence. In my heart I feel he is still close. Still here. Because of that, he still exists for me and has not really disappeared, not definitely.

Let me then trust in that, just as much as I also trust in having children too. In fact they already exist. He isn't here any more; they aren't yet conceivable. Both in a different transformation phase: No longer visible, not yet visible.

The time and the bound-to-that-body causes the impossibility of synchronism. It confines us to observing just one phase instead of all three. It prevents us from observing directly that non-material, non-physical but energetic phase. That was clear. Nonetheless, the possibility of experiencing my friend in my heart; in my eternity; still, in the same time. All-the-time. And *separation* is the illusion; the physical fata morgana that keeps invisible that which is experienced. Causes the invisibility, he thought.

* * * * *

"When I say that life is about itself, then it won't make you much wiser," his father had said that evening, when he came back to his question: *"What is life about then?"* He had proceeded with: "At best you will go and think about it." He chuckled, as it hadn't been lacking that. "What is life about then?" "About itself!"

No answer, no other question could have been more cryptic and more meaningful. Life a recycling cycle? Like a circle? Raising of awareness-level resulting in something like a spiral? One thing was clear to him;

permanent life, in the form of a continuously changing process. *Also, within the various phases of matter?* In any case, within this stage of being by the grace of physical existence; a toddler, youngster, adolescent. It still stood clearly present at the forefront of his mind.

Also, it went smoothly from the one development phase to the other, he thought. Without having to exert myself or busy myself, because possibly the next stage might not be attainable or maybe would be disappointing. Or what is current might need to disappear before what follows is able to appear.

"Different life-forms manifest frequencies of that one energy," his father had said. All at once he understood also that fear of growing old, and being old, belonged to the illusions. It was a device, an invention. Because added to it was "and they are all just as important". Of course that counted for the life-time stages of development as well. With adulthood just as important as adolescence. Nothing to long for. Nothing to be reluctant about. Differing, but equally important than young or older; being old. And how old was his father? He never heard him mention that. Just as little was said in the way in which older people refer to bygone times; for all those other fathers, a favourite subject.

I am *The* reality myself, he suddenly realised. In constantly changing shapes and forms. *Never there, always here. Never then, always now.* And he began to walk back towards the man he had left behind.

* * * * *

Quietly, he went and sat down beside the apparently sleeping man, whose face was hidden underneath the straw hat. In reality, I miss my own sounding-board as good company. Also our pleasure, he thought, dismayed by his own honesty, and not at all so much that my friend has disappeared. My sadness is about that; the loss of that. At the deepest level it is self pity, because of the 'stolen' possibility of enjoying life together. Mixed with anger at being unable to do anything about that 'theft'. About going to Canada he had unconsciously chosen not to be angry or sad about that. He had also made the unconscious choice to stick to the facts. To take them as they were instead of, as he was doing now, taking *his interpretation* as a fact. Besides, he realised, he had not missed the company and having fun with his friend at all, up until now. Not missed really, passed through his mind. They might have missed each other a couple of days or even weeks, more than once.

His memories about there and then; the past. His fantasy about there and soon; the future. These were the true causes of his feelings, he discovered.

Again, unconsciously, he had this time chosen *not* to stick to the facts. He had fantasized 'facts' around it. Really projected those fantasies. Because what are thoughts, extrapolating thoughts about happenings that never will take place, on the basis of events that happened or might ever have happened, other than inventions and interpretations that cause feelings. Just like that which takes place in dreams. Feelings, experienced as fact, were unconsciously related to what had taken place outside of him. That, instead of staying in touch with what was presenting itself within him; to be the product of his own unconscious choice.

Suddenly he seemed to hear his father speak again about judging and passing judgement. About interpretations. About the interpretation of a fact that is experienced as the fact itself. Exchanging the material reality, unconsciously, for an imaginary one. Treacherous exchanges, based on a thought process that had even caused wars.

Interpretations that are *regarded* as facts, are *experienced* as facts. But they are not, and are never going to become facts, was more or less what he had said. He had added that those interpretations are also value judgements, originating from a negative intention. Well, that looked completely right.

His friend's absence was not, this time, simply accepted as a fact. He had passed a negative value judgement about it because that, as such, went with his being '*dead*'. Dead is dead, right? How often he had heard this nonsense.

His unconsciously chosen *interpretation* of his negative value-judgement were the true causes of his feelings of sadness and anger. And that's the way it was. He suddenly realised why and excited by this discovery jumped up to go and have a piddle in the river.

"You didn't think I was asleep did you?"

He just heard it while he walked away, without paying attention to it.

He felt like an archaeologist who first wanted to examine and catalogue, as best he could, an inventory of the treasure he had himself unearthed, before showing and sharing. How could it be possible that he had only just now discovered that the choice he had made himself, unconsciously, had been decisive. Had made the decision for how he felt;. It was clear to him that what had already presented itself in his life was crucial to the choices he made, and to his reactions to whatever new events occurred.

He felt as though he had been living like a kind of sleep-walker. To have already lived so long, so unconsciously. Unconscious of himself; of the way his own mind worked. This had never been given any attention at school, not even in the biology lesson where undoubtedly it belonged. Sex education was given by a teacher who very obviously knew about it only from what she had heard from others. And because of this the subject was treated without enthusiasm or feeling, in the same tone and manner as that used in explaining a physics experiment in the nature study class.

Why, again and again, was the attention always focused on the outside, for the outside world, while the inside world represents the world inside, he had asked himself in a shocked way. Education was about how to unite myself with someone else, instead of how to do that for myself. *How to be intimate with someone outside of me when I can't do it, or aren't already doing so, with that someone within* me? That which, without my being aware of it, apparently always makes choices. Choices which determine how I feel.

And those feelings determine my actions, like whether or not I should go to university.

"*Not necessary but yes, useful*," he had said. The meaning of these words now began to take on much more weight. "*Not necessary*"? *Could that be because it was part of that false reality?* That could be it. Could it possibly be? *Why, "yes, useful"! To be able to practise something? But practise what? His conscious choice of his reactions?* Could be. *Would that then mean that what represents itself is only very relative? A fact presenting the apparent reality in the form of a building block for the true reality? That of one's own choice? The path; one's own path? A personal choice, consciously made, that creates a feeling which gives the impulse to action? Action which creates its own reality behind, or within, the apparent one? In the way that father does in his daily life?*

Questions that implied answers had overwhelmed him more and more. Just like the cold water of the stream he had lain in today before drying on the warm stones. The clear, bubbly water had stimulated his thinking. The warm rocks had stopped it and created space. The space for this very small boy's feeling of eternity. Absence of coming and going. Being one, being none. His true reality. (truly his reality)

VI   The creation

For a long time he had stood and watched the boy. Stretched out there, protected by the moving half-shade of the small birch leaves. Lying in the half-shade on his back, with one arm wrapped around the rock as if it were a loved one who had been entrusted to him.

Calmly, he too had sat in the half-shade, on the warm, smooth stones but somewhat higher up, with his buttocks, as usual, in a hollow and using a protruding stump as an armrest. The boy himself might not be naturally his but nonetheless his creation was to a certain degree. Of course, he thought, the result of the development is genetically determined – but this is not the case for the way in which the development is attained. That is largely determined by surrounding factors. And he had been alert to that for all those years. How well had he anticipated and reacted? Difficult to say. What is "well"?

By buying a house in a village instead of in a city, he had been provided with a well-ordered, caring environment on a human scale, with open people. To the village people he had, right from the start, been a small person with a name and an identity, instead of "that lad" or "one of those little ones". And that had influenced the third-most important environmental factor, that of gaining and working through, decisively and at least, the nature of experiences. And he himself had decidedly influenced the kind of experiences he had. Now, here, at this place, it was about perceptions. The way of processing positively, negatively or pragmatically. Suppression or even denial of experiences; gaining vision. *How* that works and through *what*. On that ground to let him come to self-knowledge. Self-knowledge which could grow and deepen until access to universal knowledge was granted. And with that, to experiencing the universal, eternally unchanging life energy. The knowledge of what to represent and realize in this dimension of duality. In conformity with the meaning which is not grounded in the physical world.

With the utmost care and patience he had observed and influenced his son's development: including his physically development as well as emotionally and psychological. Teaching him all sorts of things, some of which he knew that later, perhaps not even much later, would have be un-learned. Other things could await the right moment. The moment that the boy would, for the first time, get a complete view of the true nature of life; the totality of life, through close confrontation with death. Physical death, which is complementary to physical life in the dimension of duality. The dimension in which all can exist exclusively only by the grace of the opposite. Thus forming one whole, as a pair of opposites. Opposites which create the fata-morgana of two-ness.

This mirage of duality is experienced as reality by those who identify themselves completely with the physical body and the interaction of its functions; feeling and thinking. The physical body made up of 'beginning and end' and is only meant to act as a suitable '*vehicle*' for the journey of the consciousness through this dimension. He had, even as a small child, been unable to understand why getting in and out of that '*vehicle*' caused adults such great concern. Again, too, the opposites of 'joy and sadness' and above all – so absolutely, vividly and clearly – he had 'remembered', while still a very small boy, that his life, this time, would acknowledge its purpose. It wouldn't go wrong, at the last moment – whatever that might mean. Nor would he let himself be led up the garden path by stories. He would stick to the tangible reality of the valley that surrounded him as a reliable guide for his thoughts and actions.

He had wondered, now and again, whether he might indeed have coped with an earlier death, after a previous journey through this dimension – in the delusion that an ending point exists – and thus miss the passage or transition out of this dimension?. Moreover, without any real interest for that which clearly had already been created. With the help of a totally different '*vehicle*' in a different time than this personality, in this physical appearance now. It had however conditioned him into taking responsibility for the essential requirements in the life of his son.

This made him wonder how to offer the boy a maximal chance to discover that which would be impossible to pass on in any other way than by experiencing it for himself. And guard him as much as possible against indoctrination. Long ago he had decided to take the boy to this timeless place – straight after he had found a complete view of the true nature of the physical life. And that is the way it went. In the meantime, here he had been unable to sense those things that had become evident to the boy. An impression had been picked up of the pieces of a jigsaw puzzle which were beginning to fall into place. And this was only to be expected as the boy wasn't lacking in analytical ability. Nor in integrity nor in the ability to be honest with himself and thus to not fool himself.

Would the boy already have understood that we create our own reality, if not consciously then unconsciously, he wondered. That conscious choice of reaction is crucial as through that comes the possibility to choose one's own desired feeling. And through that, taking on complete responsibility for himself, with no dependency on what others find, feel, do or say. Would he already have been brought to a standstill by the phenomenon that there are two different ways of experiencing life? By managing it oneself or by delegating it to others. Let others do it or make one's own film, life-film, and project it as reality on the world surrounding him, or accepting what is offered as a concrete image. Using the head as a film-camera or as a photo-camera. Bringing "pictures" from the inside to the outside, or from the outside to the inside, was in fact the choice. He burst out laughing at the thought of holding both the photo-camera and the projector still – something that was essential for creating sharp images, that was paralleled by the need to hold the mind still, the contents of the head, when creating. The creating of an image that forms its own reality. Creating, creation. Never had he understood how it was possible to see 'the creation', to experience, to imagine, to explain 'the creation' as a situation that would be experienced as stable. As a thing, a sort of end-product instead of as the continuing process of permanent change for everyone and everything. In a complex coherence and interaction of a variety of pulsating life-forms. Hilariously funny, the idea that the creation could have a creator – instead of being self-creating. Again and again, always being pinned to the illusion of duality through finite spirits. Spirits who produce dual learning with the help of a carnal mind to which entrance can barely be achieved. And at best, elaborating on preceding thoughts but mostly only reconstructing and contesting them. Taking mock knowing-better for wisdom. Wisdom that has nothing to do with the universal wisdom in the 'enclosed' 90 percent of the brain. Nor with the consciously expressed presence of the universal, eternal, unchangeable life-energy which, if consciously experienced, can also be consciously steered creatively. Or better put, to be left space to manifest itself. Even making possible the manifestation of wisdom from the inaccessibility of one's own knowing.

* * * * *

Yet again, one of those beautiful, never understood or deliberately—in a nonsensically way—explained stories flashed across his mind.

The human being, as man/woman, as us, experiencing no duality in the effortlessness of *Being*. *Being* together. Without the necessity of 'doing'; together. Experiencing the presence of the universal, eternally unchangeable life-energy and as a unit applying that universal wisdom in complete trust. Until something goes wrong with that trust and *a choice* is made. A choice for trusting one's own 'wisdom' which exists out of powerless, fabricated thoughts, not taking any responsibility for the feeling that such thoughts cause, or for one's own actions which follow from it as a consequence.

This crucial attitude of choice, according to the Genesis story of Eve & Adam, means that, even up to the present day, people are banished from the effortlessness of *'Being'*.

Both, woman and man are trapped, separately, in a framework of *'Doing', because of* the almost complete blockage of their ability to create paradise somewhere in the outside world.

There is not, like the Genesis story, a Garden of Eden closed by their God, with a vindictive angel guarding the entrance. It is a part of our inner world that is closed off by *ourselves*, and guarded by our own centrally positioned ego. A strategically *self*-placed ego through *self*-made choices. In this Genesis story, the desire for an apple is a symbol for the eternal and crucial choice which makes all of us focus on material possessions. As a result, mankind has difficulty in accepting that one's ego has to be made subservient to an attitude of 'letting go' of desires in order to create one's personal paradise.

To experience paradise one needs to exist without an attitude of greediness or a desire to possess.

Also, this Genesis story is not just an historical drama, with the leading character being a woman playing the 'know-all' by seducing her partner with an apple. This ancient archetypal story is about a human process which has happened *daily* throughout history, up to and including, the present day.

The usual 'explanation' of this story again relates to the confinement, and the delusion, of the duality by ego-dominated spirits: spirits who are unable to distinguish and experience the human dual-multiplicity in a wholeness of part and counterpart. Making of that, in their image of delusion, two people: Man and woman. Neglecting that the feminine as well as the masculine form of the human can only manifest itself creatively by being complementary. Both physically and mentally.

Luckily his son had sensed that as well. He seemed to feel fairly relaxed with all girls, and girlfriends, giving some special attention to one of them. This, in the relaxation and awareness of equality. Respecting and being respected. Enjoying each other's sensuality and un concernedness. Exploring each other's essence in divergent situations and by doing so gaining a view on possibilities and restrictions, without being troubled too much about the advice, opinions or prohibitions of elders or parents.

He smiled after having looked at the sleeping body. *Balance,* he thought, that's what it is all about. To be quiet, *neutral.* To completely accept each other and apparent opposites, instead of bouncing between them, physically and mentally, without all the negative energy involved in making choices and judging. Bringing forth the energy that destroys and discredits closes down paradise as well. The thing is *not* to destroy. Doing the one thing with the help of the other, but *Being* – the coupling that complements the other, with the help of the other. Dare to Be the one who makes the whole visible from one's own unfettered wisdom. With confidence about admitting universal wisdom which always includes and never excludes everything. Which manifests, through the universal energy, what really is necessary. What is really needed for further personal growth and development, irrespective of whether it concerns objects, people or situations. Never ask how it is possible; just enjoy it, he had realized long ago. And with that instructed his subservient ego, which was sticking its head up, to be quiet.

The discovery; that letting go of desires and being conscious of what was absolutely necessary, made chasing this 'absolutely necessary' superfluous, filled him with awe and still did so. It had led him to regularly give some attention to what was necessary, without being attached to being scored on success. Nevertheless, success had always been granted to him. And those successes had appeared in shorter and shorter periods of time until it reached the stage where the duration between the point of becoming conscious of a real need for something, or someone, and its realization, or manifestation, took only days instead of weeks.

VII The dream

The intense heat of the dry air made her image blurred, and she seemed far away. Yet he felt her nearby. Her large dark eyes were clearly visible, and seemed to be within reach, and in spite of the distance he felt her curved form. The warm smoothness of her skin under his hand. He wondered if he was awake now or dreaming, and laughed at the absurdity of that question. Clearly he felt her warm curvature. Only dreaming that she was far away. Just like, through separation, he always dreamed about her inaccessibility. The distance between them. Even when they were together.

Proximity in inaccessibility through separation? No, through being shut out. And now, at a distance, accessible and inviting; willing to let him be close, inside those shining eyes, he felt strangely apprehensive. Wondered why those eyes attracted him and, at the same time, seemed to stop him. *Or was he stopping himself through fear? Fear of revealing himself completely?* To completely entrust himself to her instead of ravishing her?

At once he felt his foolishness in being fixated

on her body. Her black triangle. The idea, of having something to look for in there. To have expected to be able to enter into her, there. It seemed strange to him now. How should he be able to do something with a part of an unfamiliar whole? A whole of which he above all didn't dare to be part. Was her inaccessibility being caused by his notion that there was something to take?

Distance through his manoeuvring, insisting, on doing it together? Neglecting the being really together? *Inaccessibility through his inability to let her, in willingness to surrender, enter into him?* He felt himself become intensely sad from knowing that this was true. At the same time he saw his reflection in the eyes become larger and larger until they coincided with him. Confused, he realized he had seen himself. Seen himself as he actually was. Through the eyes of that other one.

The other one who never slept. Always observing him. Often let him know in the mornings that he had slept well and that he had been dreaming. Even let him remember what he had dreamed that night. Sometimes let him know during the dreaming, that he was dreaming. Creating the illusion of being awake while he was sleeping. Making it painfully obvious to him that his perception of separation and of being held away was based on his intent to take, instead of giving himself. An attitude that also caused the resistance to and his fear of surrendering. *Surrender to The other, as an other in himself? Or he himself, unchangeable during all changes?*

* * * * *

Suddenly he felt the warmth of the sun, heard the murmuring of the surf. He saw the grass around him again, waving in the wind that came over the little hill which he lay behind. About five years old. Whilst time did not exist and he felt taken up into the spaciousness beneath the blue sky. Knowing to have always been and will be part of this. In completeness, wholeness, his natural state of being. Vaguely amazed about bustling adults. Whilst all was already there, right? Or not?

The grass changed. The sound of the surf disappeared. Large clouds floated by. The small hill made way for a tent. He lay and watched that. He felt amazed, confused and uneasy. Why, he asked himself, am I really here and how come that I am alone? And suddenly: where has my girlfriend gone? Slowly the memory came back to him. The picture became sharper; they had stood up after the conversation and left. After he had said he would be together with her after having done It together. She had pushed him away from her with the words:

"I can be with you completely when you embrace me into your heart and let me into your life."
"I am not a piece of equipment that you pick up and put down when you feel like it and when it is convenient to you."
"That is inhuman."
"I don't want to be just a thing. Or just a woman."
"I want to be human. Together with you."

"Experiencing togetherness, when giving myself completely."

"Because I love you."

Did he love her? he wondered. Or did he only love, or love first of all, what he was intending to do with her?

Dismayed, he realized that he didn't even love himself enough to be able to let himself do what he would like to do. Let alone make that possible for her.

He suddenly felt cold and rather lost. He looked around him. Was he having (did he live in) a dream? Or was he dreaming away his life?

Where was he really and what was he?

VIII The meal

He had looked at it calmly, recognising the disorientation between what was what, after sleeping. Initially, parallel realities, in a certain way like the apparent and true reality are, he thought. Whereby the apparent conforms to the true when the meaning of it is experienced and expressed. And again he felt the so-familiar amazement. The amazement that this realisation had gone astray.

At a certain point, this ancient wisdom, about how to manifest true reality out of the apparent one, was no longer passed on to the next generation.

At one time, this wisdom was simply communicated through stories of what had been experienced and what had been lived through. This wisdom received full attention because it was clear that it was based on real experiences in the life of the storyteller.

However, over time the stories were no longer based on personal experience and when the spoken stories were no longer made concrete and real — by having the story-teller as a living example, as a role model — they became stripped of true their knowledge, of life's essence, and started 'leading their own lives'; as fairy tales or as gospel, or even as 'joyous messages'. Where some sort of unusual, or macabre, incident could be identified, some stories went on to become the basis of a wide range of folklore and to 'live their own lives' unconnected to the daily life shared by all.

These weakened stories, were still told, but were no longer used by fathers for the initiation of their sons; to demonstrate how to take full responsibility for their own lives as adults.

In the same way, mothers no longer used the accumulated wisdom for the initiation of their daughters to the crucial transition from 'Daddy's little girl' to 'desired woman' of someone's son.

Stories that fell into the hands of professional storytellers thus became coloured intellectually; accentuated or 'explained' on the ground of hearsay; extensively studied; much read about, or spoken about by professors. These stories were always brought into line with dogmas and self-interest and therefore could be considered to be '*dead*'. They were no longer the carriers of self-experienced knowledge and no longer be passed on and recited by those whose lives were lived as an example of these stories, in familiarity with the creative substance and the flow of creative ability.

This priceless knowledge-by-experience, which apparently had been lost, nonetheless revealed itself anew throughout the centuries, he realized gratefully. Disclosed on a very restricted scale, true enough; always vilified; always contested in the name of civilisation. But it had always, and without words, found new carriers. They were disclosed to those who refused to accept outright that the existence of one human could be inferior to that of another; or to an ideology, a nationality or some other statement of conviction from another human. Disclosed to those who could see clearly that people can't become massively unhealthy from a '*healthy*' way of living together. However, they certainly *can* get cancer, on an enormous scale in an '*unhealthy*' community, where the wellbeing of the whole means something other than the wellbeing of the individuals with names and surnames who make up that whole. Could his son be someone like this?

Recognising the voice of their hearts as authority "by grace of the gods" to whom is owed obedience in a way that common sense suggests. Would the boy appear to be capable of disclosing this knowledge of the heart to him? he wondered, as he stood up and walked towards him.

* * * * *

Without words they had stood and watched the stream until the boy began to tell about his dream. Hesitantly at first, almost reluctantly, as though it was something of which to be ashamed. But still, the whole story had come out and closed with the heavy sigh as if it was too much to understand completely.

At the same time it was also very clear. Where then lay the difficulty? he had asked. And he received an explanation. There on the bridge insight was gained to represent the eternity in time which, through this dream, had now gained the reality of one's own experience. This in spite of that gnawing little voice at the back of his head that continually said "dreams are deceit".

He had clearly recognised the present, always unchangeable, vigilant observer – in his changeable, temporary appearance – as the eternally unchangeable 'Self' that represented the whole. As well as that, the consequences from it now dazzled him, as did the effort it took not to go and rationalise; to stay in and with his own feeling.

He had been unable to reply and had only made a movement with his head that said that they should leave. While gathering their things he had mentioned in passing that the time had arrived to go to the other side of the river. There was a spot, just across the bridge, on the left hand side, where the grass was overhung by trimmed trees growing alongside the driveway, which formed an ideal place for an overnight stay. A pleasant place to cook as well, still in daylight, and where they could continue to exchange thoughts right next to the car with all the necessary supplies for cooking.

The boy had been surprised at the place. Like the way he had been surprised about the way in which this intimate place had been left free, as a terrace between the bend in the path and that of the river. Inaccessible from all sides, except from just across the bridge. It was as though a drive had been built specially in such a way that the car could be driven effortlessly until underneath the branches of the elder tree. This would act as a barrier to access and, if necessary, as a shelter from the wind.

He cut off a couple of long, prickly runners from a wild rose which was growing in the long grass and which had lain right across the place they had trodden down for their picnic. There were plenty of dead birch branches and trunks available for fuel to make a cooking fire. And although, considering the heat of the day and the dry surroundings, it had not seemed very sensible to make a fire, but he still felt a strong temptation to do so in the luscious grass of this shadowy place. It seemed that it could most certainly do no harm here. Besides, he loved the smell and the crackling that he missed when using gas. However, after a little hesitation, he acted on common sense.

Very soon a large pan of river water stood on the hissing gas burner. They could use this as the basic ingredient for coffee, soup, rice and beans and could steam some items above it. Also, the camp beds, with their head-ends close by the side of the car, were smoothly folded out, put together and covered with sleeping bags under a large woollen blanket. An effective protection against early morning cold and dew.

* * * * *

Sitting in the low, comfortable camping chairs they were lightly clad and they made sure that both arms and legs were protected against insects. The low camping table, with some left-over olives, next to the empty wine glasses, stood between them so that he could effortlessly fill up the coffee maker without moving from his chair.

He had looked at his son questioningly and the boy jokingly replied with "Yes please". Immediately after that he remarked that he did not know where to start and that, by the way, in the meantime the relativity of beginning and end had become clear to him. He had kept quiet and had nodded encouragingly to the boy while he slowly pressed down the filter-plunger. He thought with pleasure that his hand felt just the right amount of resistance from the plunger, proving that it had been pressed at the right moment, so that the coffee would have the right colour and taste. Hot, strong coffee had seemed to him, in this cooler place, without sun, a good beginning to the meal. Less suitable to finish just before going to sleep.

While the stacked pans, one of vegetable soup and on top of that the green beans covered with fast-cooking rice, stood and simmered, the boy said pensively: *"Do I live in a dream? Where and what am I, in essence?"*

He had looked down at the young oaks and birches alongside the river, a couple of metres below, while he had answered that it was just as well to take this point of view; that life was dreamed, with an option to make a nightmare of it. Then he had looked at him and added "or the opposite of that".

He clarified this with: what is experienced, or ought to be is then presented for further personal growth and development. In life's dream these incidents and events will present themselves in all sorts of appropriate forms. Like the blocks in a child's toy-box present themselves in all shapes and sizes. Offering the possibility of becoming aware in a playful way of the law of cause and effect. Developing one's own creativity through experiencing possibilities and restrictions as well as insights and skills. He pointed out that the incidents and events of life, like the blocks in the toy-box, formed material to practise life-long development – just as a small child develops through practising during the tot and toddler stages. That the goal is the practice and not the to-be-reached result of structure after structure. An adult ought to no more attach himself to an achieved result than a tot does to a tower built of blocks. By maintaining the created tower, the possibility of playing with blocks would disappear, just as 'homo-ludens' (the playing human) disappears with wanting to preserve something that has already been built, or formed 'until death us do part'. The same principle applies to wanting to preserve something that has been 'built up' until it can be passed over to a child or grandchild who, as a result, can also be made a prisoner of his possessions: and in that way also lose the possibility to gain his own life experiences in a playful way, with freedom of movement.

He had wanted to show, with these examples, that the choice of freedom and the to-be-experienced freedom with the to-be-experienced quality of life which are hidden in an individual way *How* is dealt with as it presents itself; is hidden in a conscious, or possibly unconscious way; choices are made for a reaction or approach of life-events and incidents. Possibly a conscious decision is restrained from reacting to it. A reaction is based on the starting-point being loosened up or tightened up, which leads to staying relaxed, and experiencing 'natural' happiness, or tensely running after happiness. Wanted happiness that continually seems to escape through inconstancy of that which is desired and the need to try and make it constant anyway. Like running to the end of the rainbow.

* * * * *

"I now choose consciously for the loosening-up of my coffee mug and the tightening-up of the soup-bowl between my feet," the boy had said. From the laugh it was evident that his point had been taken and moreover, understood. While he put the rice-pan back on the flame, he had carefully poured out the contents of the small soup-pan into the bowls. He had taken advantage of the opportunity to pick up the bottle and quickly fill the wineglasses so that a glass could be reached over the soup bowl and accompanied by a toast: 'To life'.

"Yes. To life! Wherever and whatever that may be," he had received back, in a pensive tone. "Life; your life, my life, is everywhere. Always, eternal, unchanging," he had answered. "Here is where our form is, our body. Where is here? It is between the 'the lines' of place and time, in this dimension of duality. During a number of 24-hour periods, within this duality, our form, our body serves as life's carrier. It is meant to manifest us, life, within that. To carry on through that duality, literally and figuratively. What is NOT meant is for life's carrier to get stuck in duality. To remain stuck in all those pairs of opposites that fascinate so, and appear to be so captivating.

"During the journey through the duality, it is always possible to be baffled by the possibility of that foolishness. Letting it captivate and be stuck within it.

The foolishness of total identification with the form, with the body, and identifying the thoughts and feelings of that materialised form as being 'life'. To experience it as 'the whole life'. An experience that then takes place through the unique *personality* of the body. This, while that personality is nothing other than the result of the way in which mind and feeling interact with each other. The personality is an electro-biochemical process which is meant to propel and steer the carrier of life. Experiencing oneself in and through a continuous changing process that offers the possibility of becoming conscious. Conscious of the true reality. Taking cognisance of the true self to which the personality is meant to be subservient, just like an operating system". During his explanation, every now and then, he had taken a spoon full of soup and a swallow of wine and it took him by surprise how immediately his son reacted.

"A permanently changing process in the material world out of which can be learned that it serves as a 'black box' for the non-material life that manifests itself in the material form with the help of mind and feeling," the boy had summed up.

"Precisely," he had answered. "You hit the nail on the head. And the most important thing: it all happens by means of inspiration; the universal wisdom which includes everything and excludes nothing; that leads to *enthusiasm*, a word that means 'en-theos', being in god."

In the silence that fell, the boy had divided the small amount of soup that remained and had established that the rice and beans were nicely cooked, without being burnt. Because he had wanted to keep it that way he had left the small pan on the burner but had turned off the gas underneath.

He remarked that personality, the ego, seemed to be a strength as well as a weakness in a human, and thus also in himself. Then, as a follow-on, he had asked how *the ego, a personality,* could *react* against others and yet also be able to *change*; and whether the personality was meant to be able to go through the changing processes or to be the vehicle to support that change.

He also referred to the dream about his girlfriend in the tent and his resistance to accepting her the way she was. His reaction against her wishes and expectations. This, while he felt the reaction of his body that drew him to her at the same time. The strange discovery of being able to experience, even to react against himself in his dream. At its deepest, not being able to accept his girlfriend but also not being able to accept himself as he truly was.

His son had by then looked somewhat helpless and had said no more while he began to dish the rice and beans, dividing the contents of the pan evenly between both plates. He even remembered the dash of olive oil across the beans, while he had asked himself how to deliver a suitable reaction. He had effortlessly lifted the lid from a can of sardines so that he could, with his knife, flip a sardine out of the olive oil onto each plate and split the last one lengthways to share it. "Don't let everything get cold," he said, and after a few bites, he refilled their glasses and continued:

"The ego, the personality, is fixed on preserving

itself. The comment that someone is egocentric is neither here nor there. It doesn't say anything about the more than usual strength of that attitude. Every subconscious human is egocentric. The extent barely differs. Only the apparent extent does. The reason for that is that the subconscious personality is, *only capable of experiencing itself as reality.*

"Besides, nature is fixed on preserving that 'reality' as optimally as possible – by way of subservience *from* others instead of *to* others. Others who after all can't be experienced as concrete, as of equal value and thus truly accepted. The expectations of the girl in the tent differed from yours and so were not experienced as of equal value.

"Your physical desire was experienced as more important than her emotional-psychic need and therefore she had to be made subservient. Both desires were probably equally strong and therefore just as important. Yet *your* desires and reactions to 'being together' felt realistic to you – and *hers* didn't.

All the same, she planted a seed in your head and heart by talking about '*experiencing* togetherness'. About '*giving* completely'; being *the female* way of wanting *to receive*. That is a frontal attack on *the male* ego which thinks only in terms of completely *taking*, instead of completely *giving*, in order to receive,

'Experiencing togetherness' is only possible when you also want to give yourself completely – something the male ego doesn't want to accept. It resists with all kind of rationalisations as soon as you start to become aware of that this is what you have to do, because connecting, unity, is the necessary reality.

The condition needed in order to be able to create. Necessary in order to be able to achieve continued existence, from a completely human perspective.

Your personality rebels against it; logical enough from one point of view as making oneself subordinate or even subservient is foreign to the nature of the ego. It thus tries to make clear to you, from the brain and feeling, that going together and being together are also perfectly possible exclusively on a physical level: exclusively as release of tension.

As a natural consequence of a natural process in which one just has to figure as necessary. The personality has a tendency to react against others, because it believes itself to be more worthy than others. An illusion that feels both virtual and real, because the ego can only experience itself as it is and because of the delusion, as worth more than others. Those others have to be made subservient, as said earlier. The dominance of the ego that is necessary for that is obtained by confrontation. Confrontation as a goal and also as a tool for goals to be reached. Goals which get all sorts of names, except the true name.

"Concerning subjection through domination: the personality also shows resistance against the other, against changing. Because changing, transformation – as the essence of the universal, eternal unchangeable life-energy – creates our learning experiences. Experiences that can lead to insights from which learning is drawn. Insights which can create awareness that leads to subservience. That is to say destruction of the ego through personality change.

This personality change occurs when awareness

of the universal, eternally unchanging life-energy
has made the person decide to open up to universal
wisdom. And thus to live again 'in paradise'. Living
the inspiration instead of consulting the corporeal
intellect with questions of 'what to Do' and 'what to
Leave'. To listen to the heart, which tells what has
to be lived, now. In full trust that the inspiration is
completely necessary for further personal growth and
development, whatever this might be. Realising as
well, never to have been able to think up what this
is, oneself, but leaving that awareness to the 'whole',
and as part of the whole making oneself subservient
to it.

"The old personality identifies itself exclusively with
self and the new one does the same with the universal,
eternally unchanging life-energy. This experiences
mind and feelings by means of universal wisdom
instead of exclusively through interaction between
those two and thus 'hearing' the voice of the heart as
'knowing'."

*"But is competition, rivalry, war, then our natural
disposition? As a kind of inborn failing or a kind of
hereditary illness?"* the boy had asked, with an anxious
face, hardly noticing that he had dropped a few beans
from his spoon into the grass.

"Yes, also," he had answered and had realised
perhaps that it might have been better to leave it at
that. Until the raised eyebrows caught his attention.
An encouragement to give more than that "also".

* * * * *

"Competition and rivalry fit 'the old personality' like a glove, because in fact they represent a war-like situation. It is not without reason that competition is called 'cut-throat'. Also refers to that: in the semifinal of competition 'they have been slain on the field of honour'. From this kind of situation emanates a very large attraction, power, because it springs from- and therefore links with, the essential quality of the ego. Reaching dominance by confrontation, resulting in subservience. Stirred up adroitly everywhere by people and organisations who, no matter what, want to secure and keep those positions.

"All of this takes place on national, international and individual, collective, micro and macro-level. Visible or invisible; it is everywhere. It is always there: the striving of ego. Competition and rivalry is, in fact, proof of lack of awareness. And the consequence of it, of *non*-awareness, is that the madness of the ego is the *true* enemy. The *inner* enemy of each human that refuses to recognise another human as equal, as an equal who also functions as part of the very same whole. Through the very same energy.

"As soon as there is insight that *the -only- true rival, or terrorist, is one's own ego*, it creates space. Space for the discovery that another way exists. A way of cooperation instead of rivalry. In that sense the present is an interesting period in mankind's development.

"In the 21st century the world population will still be able to double itself a few times with an attitude of 'homo-ludens'; the playing human being, to 25 billion, or even more than that, to an unimaginable 50 billion, by choosing to feel how it is to experience pleasure in working together and being prepared to proportionally *share* the results of that.

"By proceeding as 'homo-economistic'; we are unconsciously choosing to indirectly work against others and, by doing so, against oneself. This will obviously help to halve the world population. Even a few times, with the same ease. Just as occurred in the middle ages with the populations of many cities in parts of Western Europe.

If there is no real change in human attitudes and behaviour, during this century, soon all kind of 'coincidental' disasters will start to take place everywhere.

"Ecological, climatic, radiological, biological, epidemic and pandemic events will in that case be the inducement, *not the cause*, of these apparent coincidences.

"The underlying cause will then *not* lie in a stagnating economy or in a lack of energy or water supply, but in a stagnating development of further growth in the collective consciousness which is necessary for achieving a *massive p*ersonality-change. Instead of realising incidental changes by only a few people. This stagnating development will result in the fatal absence of a sufficient percentage of renewed personalities. Those who feel a compelling need to support the whole and maintain that in *equal* extent as themselves. Inspired to that end through universal wisdom and also appearing able to do that – Adroitly and with enthusiasm."

* * * * *

He had taken the last bite of his now cold rice and had looked up for quite a while, past the boy, at the first star. However it wasn't fully dark yet, soon many would sparkle. *"Does not such an enormous catastrophe depress or alarm you? Or are you so calm because you are convinced that it won't happen?"* the boy asked in an inquisitive tone.

"Neither," he had answered, again feeling inclined to leave it at that. And again not choosing to do so, sensing the need to carry on with the answer.

"No, it doesn't alarm me because what you call a possible 'enormous catastrophe' is not the point. Not yet. Besides, catastrophe is not a fact but your own value judgement."

"Life pulsates. It appears in life forms and disappears from life forms. At a high level of consciousness there are many and in great variety. At a low level of consciousness there are also less and less diverse. Decimations, induced by the urge to dominate and to master physical nuclear power, have occurred before. Emanated as phenomena out of the natural state of the unconscious human being. Moreover, each human can only see its own death from this dimension. For not one human exists the possibility of experiencing a multiple death."

"The scale, or the massive way in which humans physically can cease to exist, is, and remains, an experience of others. An experience, a spectacle for the laggards. Nobody can also die the death of somebody, to summarise it briefly. My other immaterial state of being, my own transition into another dimension, neither alarms nor dispirits, but intrigues," he added.

* * * * *

"But how do you see the possibility that there could be a choice for a change of system? How do you think something like that could be achieved?" The question sounded almost breathless.

"Changing of the system isn't under discussion and can't be either, because a system is a symptom. Symptom changing through system changing? That is just an optical illusion. A monster without value, as you know.

We find ourselves now, more than 6,000 years after the last time – as still survives in old folk tales – again arriving at the point that an illusion is cherished and sold, to be able to master "nuclear power". Whereupon it is unjustly claimed that this would be possible – claimed by people with the old personality. Claimed unjustly because the old personality can't even master its own psychic nuclear power.

"Mastering one's own psychic nuclear power is an absolute requirement – crucial for mastering the physical nuclear power, to which it represents the equivalent.

Mastering the safety of a process technology, or the methods of constructing a nuclear power plant, is not the issue. Nor is mastering the ultimate problem of how to dispose of radioactive nuclear waste. The crucial factor is the un-safety of our human nature. The centre point that everything turns around is the psychical social state of un-safety that persists as long as the personality change does not take place. A situation in which the ego has not yet made itself subservient to the soul.

As inside, as outside, states the law of synchronicity. The invisible brings forth the visible. It is not the outside world that needs to be our choice as the object of transformation, it is the inside world that we need to choose.

"Out of the world of perception flows the to-be-experienced world, individual and collective. Ego-transformation, forming self-subservience, lies at the root of mastering physical power and its transformation. The last time, or even other times that universal life withdrew itself for millennia, was on a world-wide scale. It is now standing on the verge of doing that again."

"It will do that, too while we unconsciously choose to continue listening to the fairy-tales of our terrorising egos. The responsibility for this unconscious choice shifting to the exponents of that – the priests and politicians – who only function as our ego-mirrors, who make the demagogy of our ego visible in the form of lying and deceiving demagogues.

"The *good* news that is enclosed in all of this, is that there is nothing that has to be achieved before a change of personal behaviour can take place. There are no dependencies, there is *nothing* that has to be achieved first, by anyone, before change can happen.

Everyone can start the process of personal change, for him or herself, by changing the way we think about ourselves:

- To no longer regard as absolute one's own life, as one's own physical form, in this dimension.

- To no longer see a personality of appearing and disappearing stature as his or her whole life.

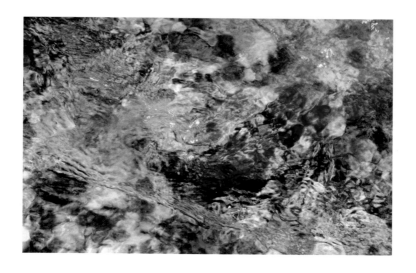

– To choose from now on to regard it as being a borrowed vehicle. One that we can direct because an operating system has been installed for the visiting soul in this dimension.

Flowing from that, each individual must not consider themselves to be more important than any other individual, and as a result of that change in thought process to no longer try to raise themselves above others.

* * * * *

The invisible brings forth the visible and shows itself as an energy frequency in a physical life form. This applies equally for 'perception' which is based upon choices. The chosen perception creates, collectively and individually, that which will be perceived in time.

The created energy model materialises, on micro and macro levels. The ancient story about the necessity of a minimal number of righteous people in a society refers to this. As long as these are to be found, life will continue to manifest itself. When a significant number of righteous people no longer forms part of society then the universal life-energy withdraws and that society disappears.

Out of those old traditions, it can be concluded that by righteous people is meant those who don't exclusively identify with the physical life of body and ego. What is meant by righteous people is those who consciously open themselves to the universal wisdom

83

as inspiration for how we can live in conjunction with the whole.

It looks very much as if that conscious choice for this opening of oneself in conjunction with others forms the *cohesion* of a society. And this makes the difference between the continuation or downfall of a society; of people. This also applies to individuals – especially them. It is significant that in this multi-millennia-old, handed down story it is all about a man with a new personality: Lot – "Fate" – and its family.

* * * * *

He, and with him his family, had created his energy model. Not against, but in favour of living together. That had materialised in a concrete way. He was given the opportunity to live on, with his family, away from destruction of cities.

The crucial point at which a choice has to be made, or unconsciously not to be made, presents itself periodically during the development of mankind. At this moment in time, it seems to me, it is doing so again.

The ancient 'screenplay' of this was regarded as so important that it remained preserved in stories in various traditions. For hundreds of generations it was told in the form of someone who continued to hold a contrary point of view while all the others degenerated.

Thus, it was told in the form of an extreme warning, but at the same time contained the encouragement. The incitement was that it was not the destruction of the physical life; the old personality, that was crucial, but the preservation of the *new* personality, with which he knew himself to be connected. That is where the emphasis lies in these stories.

That the destruction, as a result of one's own choices, could have been prevented through timely, voluntary renunciation of the old personality, is implicit and almost suggested. But still, this could have been prevented, by each one, personally. The impact and consequences of that are enormous; so enormous that they rise beyond our comprehension. Because they are not 'comprehended' they are also not experienced, or lived, by the old personality; even when lived, as a role model (for example), by a new personality. The ego desires never to be over-ruled, by anything. It also thus refuses to accept that the scope of these stories is, to some degree, too large to grasp".

He continued: "The human who merely identifies himself with his ego and doesn't 'believe' in anything more than his own self, therefore chooses to interpret these stories according to human measures. The story's human measure; an historical moralistic drama, or a natural disaster, in the category of once, but never again.

"The mind, is well able to grasp the interpretation of a screenplay, and then declare its veracity, complete with a 'declaration of authenticity' from experts at institutions which are kept going especially for that purpose – supplying explanations and additional information for professional story-tellers who know about it. Explanations which overlook the hidden core message in which every human being can be preserved from destruction by recollecting and re-internalising his true nature."

"This can be achieved simply by identifying himself with that true, timeless nature; joining himself with the inner observer and out of that connection; of living with others. To keep living and live on."

* * * * *

"It would appear that a great teacher referred to that with the remark that *'all who are prepared to lose life (of the old personality) will retain it'*. With that he urged everyone to take responsibility for one's own internal authority. "The authority that determines the interpretation of what life is, and the choices that have to be made within that life, and which are therefore linked to the acceptance of its inevitable consequences.

"He also encouraged: *'seek and ye shall find, knock and it shall be opened'* which refers to the inner world. Not to a yet-to-be-found guru as a substitute authority, or another *'father'* figure in the outer world.

"The explicit, implicit assignment is: Do it yourself. Examine your own heart. The explicitly implied promise, the guarantee even, is that the new personality will be found *in the surrender* to this heart-searching.

"What is *Not* possible to find... *Will* be found!"

Also, the promise of liberation is without reservation – explicit, absolute – no maybes.

"It shall be opened!" This is to all who want to leave that which is closed, to leave their own isolation of the ego-matter-identification: This will be granted; the opening to the link to wholeness will be granted.

"Apparently, it is about removing an *unconscious* decision of will towards separation, by taking a *conscious* decision to stop, to be carried out in self-motivation. Nobody else is needed for that. No special place, time, ritual, functionary, believe system or religious organisation is necessary."

"Do it yourself, here and now. Knock yourself back by taking a decision of will, now — by wanting to *connect* instead of being separate, through accepting that you are more than just the mind and feelings of a material body. It seems clear that what is being sought will be found directly after it is opened to you."

This youthful teacher with his new personality was, after all, speaking from experience and referred to that with: *"My kingdom is not of this world"*. No, not *only* from the outside world, the material world, which is the *seemingly* the entirety of the real world.

* * * * *

Reducing the joyful tidings in these teachings, by adopting human measures, was fairly simple. The world-shaking and almost incomprehensible message of *being creator of one's own life-reality* was too big to accept.

Therefore the fundamental truth of one's own internal authority was passed by, was given back, *projected back* on this young man:

It is he, not I, which is the authority, the creator of my life-reality. He is the one who must save my soul, not me. He has already saved me! Through his dying, my ego, my natural personality, no longer needs to do go through that dying process anymore.

* * * * *

A nicer way to save the ego from submission and destruction could not have been found. Not individually, through allowing itself to be fobbed off by this explanation. Not collectively through structurally hawking this philosophy for millennia.

It deserves the top prize, with five stars, for being the largest-ever theft, from people, of '*freedom*'. It is also the solid base in the whole saviours' belief-and redemption-of-sins industry.

The representatives of this organisation, each time massive personality changes started to go well, interrupted the process and slowed it down: contested it and nipped it in the bud.

However, much this industry of fantastic tales is subject to the law that 'appearing also means disappearing'. This disappearing is part of the duality in which all we know and create is subject to the cycle of rising, shining and then declining.

As more people lose the readiness to disown their own authority in favour of external authorities, the chance increases that the new personality will be discovered as the authority in one's own life.

The consequence of that is that the extent, importance and influence of belief-organisations, with alleged authority, will diminish and therefore can no longer effectively react again. The authority – from which their power and ability to manipulate comes from —will be increasingly lacking and indeed be forfeit.

That makes the chance more realistic that this time, with the rising flow of personality changes, these organisations will be exposed and sink like the empty shells they are. Finally, the old personality (both individually as collectively) will come to an abrupt end, either through the internal action of implementing one's individual choice to change, or through some external cause.

An intuitive turning-away from false pretensions and old lies – based on the authority of wielded power – is already taking place, with discontentment aimed initially at the latter. As a slow-starting, incremental, process of social change, still at an early stage, this attitude will become more and more widespread as individuals journey through the deepest point of disorientation, confusion and even despair, towards the willingness to face up to one's own self. Re-directing discontent with the old personality from the outside to the inside, towards that old personality, in *self-*confrontation *instead* of confrontation with others.

With that develops the need to 'search' and to find and then to 'knock so that the door may be opened'. To knock on the door of that self-built isolation cell whose imprisoning walls are made up of pre-dispositions; judgements; rules; values and delusions about (physical) restrictions, knowledge and superiority. Through self-confrontation, all of these projections can be released,

The scale on which this change becomes 'general' will be the deciding factor that will determine the quality of the future world-wide society. When the critical mass of 'justifiable ones' is reached it will result in world-wide living on, through togetherness. And then, through the self-creating ability derived from universal wisdom, a major change will occur, a re-structuring that moves us away from the present general practices of unofficial enslavement, confrontation and exploitation.

However, if the critical mass does *not* develop, we face a future that is like the old stories about socio-economic disintegration and downfall. This kind of disaster scenario may become the screenplay for our extermination.

This will result in a phasing-out of human life on a world-wide scale, through a process of drowning and starvation. All the pre-conditions for this disaster have already been effectively set in place during the second half of the last century. Although this has happened almost unconsciously it has been no less effective. And no organisation or human being accepts responsibility for those egocentric political, economic and military dogmas which have lead us to the brink of that huge instability which exists today.

IX The night

He had suggested taking a short walk before going to sleep and the boy nodded in agreement and pointed towards the bridge. Slowly, quietly, they walked towards it in the deep dusk of the late evening. After a while he heard him sigh deeply, the kind of sigh that doesn't come from sleep or tiredness, although it was approaching time to retire. Then came the pronouncement that he was overflowing with mixed feelings and harassed by a multitude of thoughts.

"Like?" he had asked.

"The thought that in past centuries physics and astronomy have been practised intensively and as a result our physical nature, the world around us, has been studied extensively.

In a way, that has led to insight, and knowledge about nature. And has also drastically changed mankind's physical view of the world. This has led to, among other things, the official acceptance of the fact that the earth is round, three dimensional, instead of flat. – contrary to the silly dogmas of supposed authority.

All that has been achieved while human nature, the energy structure of the whole human, has barely been studied. The result of that is that the pre-medieval, two-dimensional, view of humankind still persists and has still not been corrected to a three-dimensional image.

Only the functions of the brain, mind and memory, have had some attention. Evidently no one was ever kept profoundly busy with the nature and potency of human inspiration and its creative capacity.

The studied breadth of thinking, and the distance between memory and fantasy appear to have been multiplied gratuitously. As a result we have a generally accepted, psychiatric, confirmation of the two-dimensional, superficial, human nature.

Isn't all of that bewildering, after what we have spoken of today? How can it be that the crucial condition for personality change – linking with all aspects of ourselves and working together with others– is so enfeebled that the warning to '*love thy neighbour as thyself, and god above all*'? (For the sake of convenience without explaining how that has to be done; or what may be meant by 'God'), begins to look suspiciously like the behaviour you would encounter in a madhouse? *Doesn't that admonition seem like an impossible mission?*"

"This warning, or encouragement, has not, indeed, been broadly heeded throughout the centuries," he had answered. "It was experienced as discouraging rather than encouraging, because the warning, this warning, although of crucial importance, has become a cryptic, empty shape. No longer filled with explanation and information from those who were called clergymen, although they were deemed responsible to carry on a healthy spiritual life.

What may be understood by God? The universal, never-changing life-energy perhaps? Clergymen are people who talk about their god as professionals. Like something they have studied through reading about it instead of as something they permanently *experience* themselves – out of which strength they could lead a calm, self-fulfilling, loving life. They cannot provide a contribution to spiritual health and nor do they do so. They are making their kind of god *thinkable* for *some* people. They do not make their god *visible* for common people, nor what may be understood by that.

Psychologists and psychiatrists, who are deemed to carry responsibility for the treatment of unhealthy spiritual life and for the mentally ill, cannot do that either. They give no consideration, and they pay no attention, to the soul, the universal energy source of the mind that shapes its depth and height and so provides the third dimension. Hence, a lot has been said about the *conscious* choice of one's attitude – because it is of decisive importance.

Attitude is decisive for the health of both the spirit, and the body, and though that one's own existence and continuing existence. As is the need to take action and to accept responsibility for one's actions –a responsibility that cannot be stolen or delegated.

* * * * *

"No one has to wait for someone to announce that humankind does not exist just physically, but also three-dimensionally, spiritually. Everyone can, through sincere soul-searching, establish that and prove this to oneself by *living* that, here and now. By living as an awakened human being through identifying with this and enriching what is thought and felt between life's physical beginning and end. By further enriching feeling and thinking, through identifying ourselves with the ever awake, present and unchanging neutral observer, inside. The observer, which we call the soul, and which forms the true source of our energy.

It is the cosmic source and also, in reality, the source of the bio-chemical energy which infuses life into us. The soul, which manifests itself as a non-material observer and is our 'blind passenger', the stowaway, the unknown passenger on board the vessel that was entered for the journey through this dimension.

Consciously choosing a three-dimensional life means making the navigation of that vessel subservient to the driver and seeking to discover the unknown passenger, and to recognise and respect it as the owner- driver. It means that one can no longer ignore, neutralise, or deny this anymore and that one needs to choose consciously for self-fulfilment instead of external and material fulfilment. This means that it is a choice that is made directly, with full consciousness, to choose for material and non-material *nourishment* instead of stupefaction through physical and psychic filling. It means unified co-operation between observer and ego and also between ourselves and others.

This in loving understanding instead of jealousy, envy, suspicion or hatred. But not in self-sacrifice for others – that is not loving one's neighbours."

* * * * *

"It is of importance to understand that the one who is closest to us, is the observer, inside ourselves. To realise that the observer deserves the same love and ought to enjoy the same identification as our ego, with which the natural and instinctive identification takes place. Because only when the inner neighbour enjoys the same love and identification as the ego, can the neighbours outside ourselves be treated lovingly and with understanding. So inside, so outside.

The invisible brings forth the visible. One can only get to know the inner observer better in peace and quiet; the peace of nature and the 'space' that arises through the absence of doing. In Being together with the observer, without something or somebody else to take away the attention, just because it is demanded. Being alone, in the quiet energy of the still world of nature, the environment that represents the quiet strength of the same observer.

Being out of 'civilised surrounding', which have been brought forth by egos, and which represent and radiate 'ego' and through which the ego is activated and can dominate the observer.

Also in the same space is that which arises through letting go of tension, jealousy and fear of consequences for things that have been done – often quickly, in stressful situations. Being in the same space of the time taken to submit for inspection, those stressed actions and thoughts and the feelings which result, come through the observer. *Knowledge* comes through this inspection.

The personal knowledge of when, where and through what caused these strong desires, anger, fury, possessiveness, separation, jealousy, presumption, pride, cheating or prejudice. *Why* there was talk about these threats to mental health. Causes of sickness which, through by rampant growth for a long time, create visible effects on the physical body itself, and its functions.

By becoming aware of these causes of illness and by connecting them with changing attitudes, they can lessen quickly and can even be removed and prevented. As a result of that, the physical consequences may be prevented as well. Consequences that would manifest themselves, usually in the long term, in the form of depression, sleeplessness, stress, and problems with the heart, kidney, brain and other organs. These can be changed by attitude, because intention, and behaviour regarding the outer man, is positively influenced by loving knowledge of the inner being. Respecting that comes through identification with wholeness instead of division.

It appears to me that those who choose – and really work through– attitude-change, substitute Love for the ego-centric, unconscious behaviour that causes sickness, and through that are 'cherishing god above all'."

* * * * *

"Only a little more than 500 years ago the founder of modern physical medical science was born. Someone who, a little less than 500 years ago, burned the orthodox books of his medical faculty as being a colourful collection of superstition and error. They had become part of the system and were taught with complete conviction, supplied with impressive Latin and Greek names – in meaningless formulae which were nevertheless industriously memorised by credulous students. With the public burning of this 'bible' he destroyed the faith in the authority of medical science. He based this deed on medical knowledge and experience passed on by his father, and through his own scientific research.

Orthodox theological learning and books about mental health are also full of impressive names and empty Latin formulae. The ability to slam the door shut on that is now freely available to everyone; free on the basis of one's own spiritual knowledge coming from *experience* and one's own research of inner nature. Listening to the voice of one's heart instead of to the ego – or someone else's ego.

The nature and potency of human creative ability can only be known by each person through becoming conscious of one's own inner nature and one's own potent creativity. By means of one's own feeling, thinking, speaking and inspired activity. Taking action at the moment of knowing that this is what the heart prompts."

To his surprise, the boy had established that he understood that the universal, unchanging life's-energy manifests itself inspirationally in every human as an inner observer.

"Exactly", he had said.

Slowly, they walked quietly through the dark, under the bright stars, with the Milky Way bedecking the sky, to the sleeping place. There the boy had made the remark that he was not sleepy but trusted that sleep would come. He himself had the well-known clarity, the grateful realisation that his universal, eternal, unchanging existence was now personified here in the matter of this dimension, making its timelessness visible within that which is experienced as time. The realisation lightened his thoughts and feelings which were ever shaped and directed by that.

* * * * *

He had slid the cooking gear under the car and placed the chairs on their sides around the foot of the camp-beds. Next, with an eye to the possibility of nosy wild pigs, he improvised a simple barrier with dead birch trunks and branches along the sides. The boy had watched with interest while lying down, possibly thinking of it but not reacting, he had not raised the matter of possible night-time visitors, seeing little chance of that. He felt again the temptation to undress completely and, after this naturist day, to go to sleep like that. However, realising that there would be the cool hours before dawn he had put on a roomy T-shirt before sliding into his sleeping bag which should keep him warm down to freezing point. He also adopted the approved method of keeping on his woollen socks to avoid getting cold feet, and the boy had laughed a little at this. Then he discovered he had forgotten to brush his teeth. Let me rejoice in the exception to the rule, he had thought. That feels a lot better than being annoyed about forgetfulness. After all, the situation itself is less important than my, consciously chosen, reaction to it.

And so he had gone to lie upon his bed, looking with wide-open eyes at the stars.

Then, time and distance disappeared. He saw them all around him, as though he was one of them and one with them. He experienced the slowly approaching white contrail of a passing jet as a violent intrusion, the sight of a satellite passing by as an absurd tool flying about. This kind of pollution caused a feeling of sadness which brought him abruptly back to his camp-bed. Without understanding the reason for it, this sadness turned to anger, accompanied by a strange sort of pain and a vague realisation of the need to take responsibility of some kind here; to be jointly responsible.

The message had, very slowly, got through to him: jointly responsible, unintentionally and unconsciously, for the start of a process of thoughtful developments; a development concept which had brought forth river-pollution, air-pollution, space-pollution and, as a grand finale, even objective-pollution and *unclean thinking*. It was something that, through structural dishonesty, manifested itself in the pollution of communication and in the already visible pollution of the social and economical structure which led towards economic disintegration.

High time that our much vaunted civilisation should take civil action, he had thought; preferably by more than a handful of people in a boat, or in temporary action-groups.

High time that 'healthy ambition' should be revealed as camouflage for concealing unhealthy behaviour, often with environmental abuse and polluting consequences for all, and supposed advantages for a few.

Time that, at last, a totally different and more natural development concept should be applied. A concept based on the integrity and inviolability of the human habitat, to bring into being a Sacred respect for our polluted, poisoned and already climatologically disturbed planet. A concept that is aimed at the development of the *inside world* instead of the outside world. An action that must be undertaken world-wide by all concerned residents of the planet.

* * * * *

He must have fallen asleep as all at once, the moon was there and the positions of the stars seemed to be different. He asked himself what could have woken him up but looking around he could not spot a possible cause.

The ever-present sound of the river was the only thing to be heard. The silhouette of the elder and the trees along the river were unchanged. The deep dark-blue of the sky somewhat lighter. The top of the large woollen blanket a bit moist. His legs somewhat less warm. But that was all, he had thought. Luckily no sign of wild pigs and he had found, contentedly, that the camp-bed had proved to be remarkably comfortable for such a simple aluminium and canvas construction. Also, that blanket had proved incredibly effective against morning dew and cold.

* * * * *

"When one can die suddenly while in the middle of a conversation and if one is only eighteen, then tell me what is life about?"

This suddenly shot through his mind. Again he had been amazed about all the times he himself could have 'just' been dead. Maybe even ought to have been dead, but still appeared to be alive.

He remembered when he too was eighteen years old and his appendix, falling to pieces, had been removed just at the very last moment. Had he been scared when the emergency operation that midnight had saved his life just in time?

He remembered too when he was nineteen and had to jump off his motorcycle at 100 kilometres an hour to avoid being squashed like a fly in a head-on collision Had he been scared when, having been unconscious for three-quarters of an hour, amazement at still being alive turned into devastation to be even almost unhurt?

Had he been scared to die at twenty years of age when, quick as the lightning itself, he had shut the gate in a steel fence, right in front of a white-hot lightning ball rolling towards him, so that it rolled right past instead of against him?

Had he, at twenty-one, and just married, been scared when flying around the corner with that first, oh so small car? Or even a year later, after the startled awakening behind the steering wheel, after having worked at nights? Also, the time that this had happened on a verge, close to the eye-level, steel-pipe railing of a bridge. Or all those times in his later life, when everything that was humanly possible had gone wrong and he wasn't even hurt? Especially that time

– because his intuition had been warning him to keep much more distance from the one in front of him than usual – when he appeared to be the only one who came undamaged out of that tunnel, after being enclosed between two huge chains of car collisions, with several people trapped in their burning vehicles?

It appeared to him that fear had never played a part, but not due to a lack of imagination. Perhaps he had always unconsciously known himself to be eternal, only able to lose his body and mind.

He had turned the question round and round, like a cat with a just-caught mouse. He seemed to grasp the boy's question and still there was something of his own life there, through which he understood the possibility of missing the point. Not to have picked up what the real perception of his son had been, when that question had arisen.

"What is life about then" or *"what then is it about in life?"* was a question with very different connotations. "About itself" would be the right answer to that. But how was that question asked, exactly?

"What then is it about in life, when one can be suddenly dead, when one is only 18 years old?"

How had he himself experienced that, at that age? When he himself, also just like that, could have been dead suddenly? Not theoretically, as a spectator, but practically, as a result of a so-called diagnosis by a conscripted corporal of the medical service. "Having a temperature", of more than five degrees above normal. Not knowing anymore how to lie and writhe with pain, for hours on end without the possibility of help and knowing that it would go wrong.

It dawned on him that this was simply accepted as a fact. Also, when he had jumped off his bike, true enough without pain, it had been decided in just a split second, in a '*Go Back to Start or Take a Chance Card*' situation; without fear or emotion. Now it was clear to him; "*what is it about then in life?*"

Answer: To learn to see and learn to live. That death forms part of that, instead of being added to it at the end, as an end buffer or 'resting place'. Also to learn that death may be lived through, even has to be, *by voluntarily letting go of personality, the ego, during life.*

He had realised he had rebuilt the boy's question, asked from the boy's own perception, to accommodate his own perceptions. Also, he had suddenly understood that the boy had experienced death, at a *personality level*. Whereas, he himself always did this at a *soul-level*.

He looked beside him and saw that the continuation of this conversation would wait for a while yet. Wondering to himself how the boy would regard his friend's letting go of his body and personality now. How he would experience that now, after the first grief, fear and anger and whether he would have got through to the instigator of those vehement feelings and identified them.

Surprised, he had realised that he had come here for that but had not really spoken of it any further, as such. Also, the boy had not returned to the question or carried on about it, which indicated to him that the moment at the bridge had been well chosen? It also told him that later it would have been well worked through while on the bridge as well.? What a paradox, he thought!

Life lives and created us, as humans, in this dimension. We maintain the collective delusion that it is we, people, who grant life, have granted life to someone. The delusion that we experience and create our life, ourselves, and can, in our own way, design it, and even prolong it, or, if desired, shorten it. Although the facts are simple the understanding of them is so much more difficult. Death, unjustly interpreted as something finally to have to undergo – as a sort of punishment – has to be postponed as long as possible.

And also, every given 'explanation' of those simple facts is clouded by the pollution of thoughts brought on through false convictions and do not add any clarity at all.

* * * * *

In a society that, without further ado, accepts that those who pass themselves off as guides in the esoteric field are indeed that, interpretation at a human level is accepted as being the factual situation. But that is not the full extent of the issue: the quality of those guides is neither discussed nor denied, despite the fact that they are structurally misleading and deny of the existence of the esoteric field.

How far can it go, blindly trusting external authority instead of searching ourselves? by researching one's own inside world. What a hilarious idea. To want to name, localise, annexe the universal eternally unchanging life-energy in its universal, self-creating wisdom as from and for this planet. Again that dualistic, limited thinking.

The materialistic in the visible – and immaterial, in the invisible – sphere of *this* planet. That, while one light-point, visible low at the horizon, if that were to be hollow, could offer enough space to let the earth and, 350.000km away, her turning moon, to turn around together. Universal life-energy, which incessantly creates a universe with 'light-points' like this and like myself, does not let itself be imagined nor, he realised, personified by anyone. It does, however, let itself be experienced by everyone so that every attempt to try and imagine it is also superfluous.

How had the boy said that again? Studying the external universe had led to the discovery that the earth is not flat – not two, but three dimensional. He had also wondered why the *internal universe* had not received that same level of conscious attention. The non-physical structure of mankind was still seen as two-dimensional with the human spirit as its soul.

Why had the human spirit not been distinguished as an intermediary between the brain and feelings of the mind and the soul.

The true intention of the observer influences the perception of all that is observed. And even the observed itself, he had thought; while the image of a broken hologram again appeared to him. Ego sees ego, because is mirroring itself. Expects to see ego and then sees that too, when it goes and studies itself.

* * * * *

One of the founders of psychiatry did that: concluding that the creative energy of the ego; the sexuality, was the most important cause of behavioural and personality structures. The sexual energy as source, driver and incentive of the soul? In this way he plummets into the pit of circular reasoning. The human mind originating from physical feeling and physical brain is 'motivated' by physical bio-chemical processes. Ego, which is steered by hormones, brings itself forth; is supposed to multiply itself. How can that which is generated by the physical be named as not physical?

Through this, the language of the people, the existence of ghosts, can be ignored by saying 'ghosts don't exist', and appreciate the existence of the human spirit in the material world with 'the human spirit is ingenious'?

With closer contemplation, it is clear that the physical, electro-energised spirit is indeed derived from all which is quantitatively of importance in the bio-chemical processes of sexuality, resulting in various forms of personality behaviour. However, it does not do this qualitatively.

Our mind, in experiencing the non-physical melding together; receives spirit and inspiration. And with this, her enthusiasm. Her en-theos, being-in-god; and core quality.

The more-than-physical energy results in more than a procreative ability; real creativity. The ability to bring about *creations* and bring about *relationships* that aren't aimed exclusively at self-maintenance.

When the thinker examines his thoughts or the

dreamer his dreams, this then excludes the internal observer in the thinker or dreamer. This happened to another of the founding fathers of psychiatry.

From the illusion itself, *to be* that observer *instead* of the observed. Through this, the third dimension remains invisible. As the observed does not connect itself with his observer, the whole cannot be observed; cannot be experienced.

When the observer only looks around, and not upwards or downwards, the earth is flat and without substance. So it is with the human mind also – Stranded in philosophy, theology, psychology and sociology, so the dualistic, apparent instead of true reality.

In fact, it is all so simple, he had thought. Would this truly not have struck anyone before, during the last millennia, except for those few enlightened spirits who were barely understood, or not at all? And to what extent would the boy already have gained a view of the truth in, or behind, the apparent, he wondered.

* * * * *

Initially he had thought that it was imagination. After the slowly pushing aside from left to right, where the stars disappeared behind the mountainside, as it became less and less dark, due to the turning of the earth. Never had he seen this so clearly, so visibly as now. He had gone on to realise that the apparent flight of the stars – through his own moving along with the turning earth – formed a striking illustration. Mother earth was instructing him here, on this so magical place, giving him illustrative tuition. Instruction about the third dimension of the human mind. As with a slide show, made visible for him, that the appearing and disappearing of the inner observer was just due to the physical movement into that lively, fleshly, thinking and so busy body.

But the always awake, ever-present, unchangeable observer would not disappear suddenly, like those stars are able to disappear. The illusion of disappearing was only created by one's own movement and the disturbances caused by the coming and going of thoughts.

And doesn't the earth turn quickly, he had thought with surprise: talking about the concrete proof of cooperation and energy – universal life energy! And this is just one, small planet. Then again came the picture of the inner observer, like the still, always present, waking one. The one that stands above everything, constantly thinking and feeling: like the starry sky that always stands above the earth. In the same way that the stars are still there when the light of the sun makes their light invisible, it can only show itself in suitable circumstances.

Although not yet visible, the light of the rising sun had already made that of the stars disappear.

He slid out of his sleeping bag and carefully stepped off his camp bed to go and piddle and then went off wash himself in the river. A glance at the other bed revealed only a blanket, so he had left the toilet things in the car, thinking that teeth are better off being brushed after, rather than before breakfast and he could always dry himself with his night-shirt.

* * * * *

Above the mountainside at the end of the valley, the delicate pink of the sky promised yet another warm day. When he had been by the river he had thought that it was almost as though the mountainside had been put there just for sunrises like this, as he saw the sun come out above the lowest intersecting point of the mountainsides.

* * * * *

The valley truly was positioned fantastically. That could be seen by the few village ruins half-way to the top of the south slope. Impressive in their simplicity and solidity, although now partially decayed. Their natural stone walls were still held together by clay and although some of the slate roofs had collapsed they were, nevertheless, still serviceable shelters, even though used just for horses, not cows anymore. There were also a few houses still in occasional use, but not during the winter when it would be barbarically cold: especially in January, when the sun spent the whole day behind the mountains and never reached the valley.

Here, during the winter a metre of snow was the rule, almost without exception. Once, thinking he was heading off for a nice walk to a mountain hut, he discovered to his surprise, when he had investigated, not just one little house but the whole ruined village that it was a part of, past being preserved.

Surprised, and with growing respect, he had explored

along the many levels of terraces and metres-high walls around them. He had seen the now abandoned and collapsed animal shelters; the open stables half in the mountain's slopes and underneath or partly behind the houses; half decayed wooden tools and parts of stables. Beams from roofs or window frames, with the forged nails still in them, bore witness to craftsmanship, patience and devotion.

The enormous knowledge and experience had also impressed him. Eloquent evidence in the way in which walls more than 40cm thick had been built of surrounding rock debris, stacked and joined, like pieces of jigsaw puzzles, to provide a stable and strong whole. And with no two stones of the same shape and size.

Time had taken its toll and the timbers of the roof ridges had gradually mouldered and decayed and finally collapsed. Little strokes fell great oaks. As water had entered the buildings it had slowly washed away the clay that bound the stones together and had created the breaches in the walls.

He had tried to imagine the daily lives of these people and that had brought his thoughts back to his earliest childhood, as a little boy in the countryside; in simple splendour, halfway through the 20th century, still living in a way that had remained almost unchanged in the previous hundred years. Without running water, electricity, gas or flush-toilets. With one oil-lamp and a few oil stoves for cooking. Ready-to-use beds in cupboards along the walls of the one and only living space and the only water available in the vegetable garden, in a deep well, with a little bucket at the end of a very long rope. Outside, around the corner of the very small house, the only private space; with a smelly bucket underneath the plank with the round hole and the ready to use pieces of old newspaper on top of it. Outside also, next to the only entrance of the house, the row of tall blue and grey stone pots with wooden lids that contained salted food and vegetables like peas and different kind of beans. Also green peas and white beans together, called 'little children in the grass'. And every year, during late autumn, the preparing of bacon. His step-father providing this winter food, by the cutting of the (by then grown up) pig's throat and the storing of the salted meat in one of those big stone pots.

He thought of a life in these mountains, of sleeping when it became dark and working as long as it remained light. Working to be able to eat. Eating to be able to work. A natural cycle and a basic part of life; in connection with rocks, plants and animals, which provided all that was necessary for housing, feeding and clothing; in which new life appeared without fuss, existing and then disappearing, peacefully, in the same way. A life in which the winter months formed the natural resting period, which was spent down in the valley. Rest months that passed by calmly, looking after cattle, tools and family relationships.

* * * * *

The river had appeared colder at this early hour than he had expected. Up to his knees in the stream, he had decided to leave it at washing his head and body, scooping water over them with both hands instead of submerging himself, full-length, in the water. Experiencing the sparkling coolness as pleasant and feeling completely refreshed, he hadn't been able to resist the temptation of wading further through the river. Later, walking back along the bank, waving his wet T-shirt, he had answered the greetings of the boy, who was busy folding up the camp beds and spreading out the sleeping bags next to the blanket that was lying to dry.

To his delight, the pan with oats, raisins, dried apricots and prunes, in soy milk, already stood simmering on the quietly hissing gas-burner. The cafetiere too was already charged with coffee and just needed water. He must have got up right after me and he certainly hasn't let the grass grow under his feet, he had thought, as he walked slowly towards the scene.

While putting the chairs upright, tidying up the dead birch branches and putting away the camp beds in the car, the boy had asked him to fetch some more water from the river so that it could come to the boil during breakfast. He willingly obliged, and on his return the bowls stood, steaming with porridge, on the camping table, filled to the brim and crowned with a generous teaspoon of honey.

"Slept great", the boy had remarked. "Hardly lay awake at all! Didn't dream at all." And with a wide smile: "Slept as though it was meant to be, being homeless."

He put the kettle on the burner, turned the flame higher and carried the chairs to the other side of the car, to the long grass that had already been reached by the approaching sunlight and from where the imposing view could be enjoyed – the old concrete bridge, the trees and the river against the all-embracing sloping green scenery. The boy had thought it a good idea also and had followed him with the small table on which stood the bowls and cafetiere. While they were enjoying breakfast he had noticed his son had even added a good pinch of cinnamon to the porridge, something which to him always made the difference between just porridge and a tasty breakfast – a thoughtful touch which he appreciated.

Exactly at the moment the sunlight reached them the kettle had whistled at them. He indicated he would take care of the coffee and poured the water very slowly, after having waited a little after the first dash. The boy had inquired with interest how he had slept.

"Fitfully," he had answered. "In a more or less half awake, half asleep, state, conscious of a few things. The way this happens to me at this place, during the day as well as at night. This time it concerned the way of living with death."

"When you say it like that, do you mean that exactly," the boy had asked, "or do you mean the much spoken of- and described, life *after* death?"

"Life after death," he had replied, "does not exist. What exists is life. Life which implies, incorporates and therefore also manifests death. A process of manifestation which undoes the personality, the 'I'. The process which finally abandons, once and for all, the 'vehicle' to recycling. Even though that in itself can require some time. It is taking it too far to conclude that the physically based personality would be able to continue to exist away from the body. No. After death, let go of it. To the contrary, life that exists manifests itself also in the personality *—and vice versa* through the loss of that."

And he had suggested that after breakfast they could continue to exchange thoughts about this, while on the horse-track.

X   The path

Although it was not yet very warm, they decided nonetheless to leave their clothing, with all the other gear, in the car and had set out wearing only shoes. His father had answered the question as to where the bridle path ran to with a wide swing of his arm, thus indicating that he knew but seemed unable to explain.

So they had walked over the bridge, having crossed the path into the meadow, through an opening in the fence which he had not noticed the day before. A stone wall had presented an opening behind some bushes which gave them access along a steep path to the first terrace.

About 15 metres above the meadow they had just crossed, they saw it, tens of metres wide, stretching out for more than a hundred metres along the slope. It was as though a bright green carpet that had been laid out towards a pair of majestic hazelnut trees which grew at the end, the boy had thought. He found it remarkable that they should just grow here. What a rich harvest of nuts those trees, or rather gigantic bushes, would yield in the autumn.

Although he had not been able to see the path, some old horse droppings had caught his eye – droppings which had not seen anywhere else.

They made their way along, slipping easily from one terrace to the next, his father apparently following an invisible path. Was he discovering the path as he went or had he already walked it so often that the path had led him along, he had asked himself silently.

In front of them, a sort of alpine pasture full of flowers in many colours unfolded. Above the flowers fluttered butterflies in a variety of forms, formations and patterns. Then sloping back towards the river over which a small concrete bridge with a rusty railing offered an unexpected opportunity to explore the slope on the other bank. He had hesitantly remarked that the sun in the meadow had become so warm that he would rather like to go to the river. His father had nodded approvingly and had gone on ahead.

Carefully, precisely, he found his way through the wet part of the meadow. Through a great number of small pools and streamlets which had seemed impassable, then through the dry part in front of the bridge.

It was here he had realised that he had become a practising naturist, and that this had occurred in a completely natural and unnoticed way at one with his natural surroundings.

To be enjoying the tepid wind around his body and the optimal freedom of movement. Again the feeling of wonderment had come over him. *How well did he know his father, and how well did he know himself?* His mother had dissociated herself from naturism without ever having practised it. Nonetheless, she had spoken critically of it on several occasions.

Because of her, he suddenly realised, he had been influenced and had seen naturism and being alone or together with others in the freedom of nature, as a peculiarity of his father. And so unconsciously he had made his mothers prejudice his also.

Unbelievable that he, based on nothing but this, had made clear to his father, with great decisiveness, that he was unable to believe that life without clothing could give an enriching experience.

A few times, he had brushed aside his father's invitation to at least prove to himself this point of view. He now understood that vague smile, and the almost unnoticeable lifting of that one shoulder, with which he had taken the refusal without reply. This was the same reaction which his mother had received after her half-hearted attempt at discussion. The non-verbal reaction of someone who knows how to experience paradise.

He who knows this does not have to clarify it to those who wish to banish themselves from this. A self-chosen banishment in the illusion of separation by always wanting to put something between himself and another and then maintaining it as a frame of reference for the ego. Showing, by that very action, the inability of leading one's own life on the basis of bare facts. Preferring to live with the concealment of the created self-image and with the interpretation of the facts as fact!

How had his father once said this? It had been something like: In life, sooner or later everyone will have to come to the conclusion that they want to live in self-orientation instead of object-orientated. He had somewhat laughed about that and remarked that he still found it of some importance what those 'objects', his friends, said about him. Also, especially, how they judged him.

Nonetheless, his father, always decisive, had said that the true importance was how you judge *yourself*. Whether you can say to yourself, even when completely contrary to all other opinions, that you did that well, or not, even while others do find it so.

Does that also have to do with not going to church now anymore? he had then asked. Whereupon the cryptic reply was "churches are tombstones". And after some insisting received the confirmation that all those buildings could very well be seen as commemorative monuments to the fact that the lofty knowledge of the eternal universal life was ever practically lived. At the time he had experienced this as puzzling, as indeed he had found the remark at this morning's breakfast that "life *after* death does not exist".

Although he had been able to understand this one, (because it matched up with his own insight of the previous afternoon on the bridge), the understanding of the added; "and vice versa", had allowed itself to wait until later. Life exists and demonstrates itself in the personality as well, *and vice versa*; through the loss of it. It was said just like that. *Did not this imply the enrichment of life, the soul, with all the consciously learned lessons obtained from experiences?*

But then, he had certainly realised for himself, by obtaining these experiences, the personality had acted in a subservient interaction with the soul. In that case, the substance of the personality, or the fruit of that, would certainly continue to exist on a non-material level.

He had wondered if the talk of an 'eternal life' would refer to that? Or would that be the result of wanting to reduce the universal eternal unchangeable life-energy to human measures? And wanting to personify that? How had his father referred to the vehicle for this dimension and the operating system?

Whatever: when the soul boarded that vehicle it could make the intended journey through this dimension. Then he could imagine that the soul which was enriched with the impression of the journey could continue on.

However, so would the vehicle, through the arrival at the destination and would performing as such, have satisfied his intention? Not having got stuck on the road somewhere as a monster-without-value. And that journey can lead, in the process, to loving in equal measure that 'fellow creature' *inside,* as ones own ego. This realisation shot through him. The bringing into practice of the human 'free will' to choose, to live in self-connection instead of -disconnection. *How* he had experienced that himself, yesterday on the bridge?

Ah yes; eternity presents itself on behalf of me, in time. Naturally. Eternal life IS. Life *Now*; in myself. Myself in that, not later on. Not after a death. Not eventually.

Just as with this being in a paradise-like surroundings and in a paradise-like state. Paradise here. Adam, himself. Not searching for paradise somewhere and waiting to be admitted. Shape the paradise yourself, through your own choices and own behaviour. Behaviour which causes that feeling, a paradise feeling; which causes experiencing paradise; here and now. When that is not realised here and now, that simply means never, shocked, he had realised himself. There is but one life and that means one eternal now.

Time is not a fact: this was slowly being revealed to him. It is a subjective form of perception of *now*. It is like a river, which conveys everything that appears and takes care that, even things that are barely present, disappear again, to make room for something else that will also pass by again.

He who experienced this in that way had 'passed on' himself, more than 1,500 years ago, but at that time he had nevertheless already hit the nail exactly on the head. He felt that clearly while he stood next to his father on the primitive bridge, looking at the bubbling water between the rocks below this concrete bridge.

* * * * *

From the bridge, they had walked back into the meadow, leaving the opposite side for what it was. Then along the river which each time they entered it surprised by its depth. After nearly every bend a new vista was revealed, until his father finally brought him through the shrubs to a protruding peak. Any explanation would have been superfluous.

Apart from the waterfall, high and wide in the river,

four smaller ones fell to the blue-green pond beneath him, each entering at a different level from the other. The pond was deep and yet so clear that the stones on the bottom were perfectly visible.

After a while his father had declared it to be one of his favourite places. Even so, he had stood up shortly after with the remark that, considering the temperature today, he preferred to go and sit on the rocks *in* the river, instead of above them. Not so long after that, the path ran back down towards the bank.

They climbed carefully over the barbed wire that separated them from the river, took off their shoes and walked into the river and over to the great grey stones that were spread out in the middle, like huge pebbles.

Lying more or less next to each other, stretched out on the warmer stones, just separated by a small rapid, and with their feet in the cold water, his father had asked him whether being in the valley had given him some more insight on the different aspects of life.

That question had seemed somewhat odd to him, as he felt that his father knew very well that the answer to that would be yes. So he had given himself a short break by remarking that the bridle-path had not really seemed to be a clearly marked path, apart from traces of manure.

"Ah", was the answer; "where one goes there is a path, even when it does not appear to be so. Not only here but everywhere. Not only for horses or for me, but for everyone who does what the heart now prompts him or her to do. The *How*, always looks after itself and in a manner which differs for everyone".

After that, it had really been his turn to reply and he had said he understood that *reality* is in fact *only now* – the present. *Now* represents *the real* reality. "Exactly", the man had said and had asked him next what this actually implied.

That had seemed to him the ideal moment to say that he really did not need to go to a university to qualify for later on. That comes down to the fact that there is nothing to be achieved at all.

There are other things to be had in life: being here, being connected with all the different aspects of oneself and the people surrounding, is in fact what it's all about.

This time his father had responded: "Precisely".

But then, you do agree, Dad, that I do not need to go on studying? he had asked, astonished. "Precisely", had sounded for the second time and the man had smiled at him in that exceptional way which had always made him feel so special and happy. Now, too, that gave him a light-headed feeling, even through his astonishment.

Next, it was explained to him that studying in itself can not be good or bad for someone. That it is one's own perception of studying that takes care of a good feeling or an ill-at-ease feeling. That it is essential not to study from a 'wanting-to-have' or 'make the best of a bad job' mentality. Experiencing pleasure at studying must be the true objective.

Everything that might follow out of that and further, will take care of itself. Not a single worry is necessary, because the universe will always show exactly what is truly necessary for further personal growth and development. Possibilities would thus cross his path which he would only welcome. Which he would *have* to welcome if he wanted to make the best of them.

In pure amazement, he had almost fallen into the water. He then continued to ask how to answer the famous question: *Do you think you can earn your bread by that?*

"Meant to keep you out of your fantasy-world", had been the short answer, which, all the same, he had understood instantly. Indeed, up until then he had not given any attention to his own interest and qualities in relationship to his possibilities. Had let only a vague kind of fantasising come in place because of that.

Why could he suddenly see it as being crystal-clear now, he wondered to himself?. Because there is no longer a reaction against the present? No longer a reaction to his father and particularly... no longer a reaction against himself, or his intuition? Was this happening now through this valley, through this river, through all those trees on those so-green mountain slopes? What was actually happening here?

After he asked the question out loud, it was said that he had gone away from the *resistance* against that which presented itself in the outside world and now, because of this, change could take place in his own inner world. That the gentle energy of this very splendidly situated valley in which a natural balance still prevailed, has probably let him be a part of the biotope and experience that balance also.

* * * * *

How this balance took shape, here in the midsummer night of the longest day, as the moon went down in the very early morning, not long before sunrise, precisely at the intersection point of the mountainsides of one side and the sunrise which shortly after that happened; also above the opposite lowest intersection point at the other side.

Through the trees, first of all, which play a stabilising role in this balance. A role which in the rest of the country, especially in the south, was already absent. But luckily, in these northern border mountains, still in evidence.

Also through the thousands of litres of groundwater that all these trees individually evaporate, on a warm day, providing regular showers which keep the rivers filled and everything green. And also of great importance for the winter snows.

In fact, the unbridled felling of trees on countless mountain slopes in the rest of the country is the true cause of muddy reservoirs, empty riverbeds and the forming of deserts. The combined effect of the destruction of countless micro-climates has been at the root of the change in the country's climate.

Some decades ago, on a certain large island in the North Sea, a plantation-law was enacted to give tax credits and grants to subsidise re-forestation. The result was that the big landowners re-forested up to 20 per cent of their estates. These islanders had ample experience of the consequences of de-forestation and had learned, first-hand, how climate change felt. In the second decade of the last century they learnt within the short space of four years that they were not just squandering a whole generation of men but also destroying one-third of the total forest area of their country simply to produce 'trench timber'.

On those grounds, they have now put into action a plan to restore the balance that will, in time, improve and even safeguard the supplies of fresh water – something especially necessary for the south of the country which literally dried out for a couple of summers, and even now is still thirsty.

Through lack of geographic, historical and also biological oversight, trees were not recognised as important stabilisers of climate and freshwater supply Unfortunately, the short political life-span of policy-makers in most countries exacerbates the situation because they rarely seem to learn from each other's experiences. The political will for the delivery of a re-forestation effort only starts to develop after it is *compelled* by experiencing what it feels like. The consequences of clear-felling, precipitated by opportunism and short-sightedness, are threatening to make those parts of the country uninhabitable.

A recovery of balance, however, needs an incubation time of almost half a century and this makes re-forestation politically so unattractive that it is usually action groups who have to push the issue of decision-making. They have to compel a willingness to invest in this.

* * * * *

After listening to the whole story from the man next to him, the oppressed feeling of yesterday returned again. Again the image of screaming chainsaws, day after day, biting into the lungs of the earth returned to him and after he told his father about it he then asked the question about long term consequences:

"What did he expect to occur as a result of all this?"

"Consequences that will be socially and economically disrupting for the population of the whole world", had been the answer. Then followed: "Each tree, each large-leaved tree, can evaporate up to 10,000 litres of water in a single day. Water that has been pumped up from a depth of anything from one to several metres, and all the energy for that comes from light; from sunlight energy transformed by the tree.

Trees & forests also have to be considered from a economic perspective and although this example represents every large tree, it shows that it has a basic *economic* value that is at least the equal of a maintenance-free pumping installation: An electric motor, pipes, filters, electronics and solar-panels, which would have to be there to provide capacity for that kind of water production.

In addition to this they are FREE, natural, carbon dioxide converters –especially the deciduous trees. The forests can be seen as the primary channel of transport, between the soil, the earth, and the sky for transporting *rainwater and carbon dioxide* back to where it came from.

They are a vital link in the recycling chain. All that water is brought out of the ground back into the air and then falls on the earth again as rain or snow. Through this, all kinds of things can grow and develop; like rice, vegetables, fruit trees, rivers and us; people.

In a primeval forest the air is humid and it rains copiously and regularly. In a desert, after the forests have been felled, or burned, the air is dry and it seldom rains. There are mountain valleys in Bolivia which are as dry as dust while one valley further on there can be water in abundance. And remember that not so very long ago, none of these valleys had an aridity problem. This was *before* the inhabitants felled the trees in order to make their valley 'more habitable'.

By doing that, they broke the recycling chain. The missing link stopped their supply of water and the result was a drought that made their valley uninhabitable. Thus the life of trees appears to be inextricably bound up with the lives of people. Mutually dependent, equally important and deserving of equal respect.

And so it works – just like those Bolivian valleys – with islands, countries and continents. The only alternative, in the ultimate case, is to move away or die. How many people can live in a desert? Why is the worlds largest oil supply under that desert? It proves that abundant plant growth was once there, with plenty of fresh water. Whole primeval forests have grown there for a very long time. Just as we can still see today in areas of virgin forest. However, as more of that is both legally and illegally burned and felled, the more unstable the world climate becomes.

Rain-forests have been dampening the shocking peaks and dips of the *macro*-climate and until recently have been preventing the violent results of these movements. Now, however, the rain-forests have already become too small to be effective in that function. They are also enormous containers of carbon dioxide and this becomes hugely significant if they are demolished and that carbon is released.

The result of these unexpected and unforeseeable irregularities on the great peaks and dips of climate variation will translate for each country as agricultural disasters, together with the matching financial damage and *scarcity of food*. A phenomenon that is already fully at work. With, as the most extreme consequence, a reduction in the population. This, in the first instance, by choice... but not for long. It is high time to look at trees as part of our living, co-living heritage as occupants of this earth. To see that they are our most important and most loyal supporters. In fact, in the first instance, functioning as donors for 'the club of six milliard'.

It is time to look at trees not just 'things': things which could stand in the way or could be just providers of wood and financial profits, but as co-occupants which we must cherish like ourselves. If only because, when they largely disappear from the earth, we will also disappear: Massively destroyed. Just like those inhabitants of Bolivia who disappeared from their valley, every single one of them. When the trees went the people also went, out of their clear-felled and therefore uninhabitable dry valley. Or in this country: Trees gone, water gone, agriculture gone, tourism gone. And with that, the right to exist of all the population, gone!

This small scale Bolivian disaster perfectly illustrates the *world-wide* consequences of *exactly the same devastating felling process,* by timber-robbing, 'quick money' making companies. These have already been in operation for more than half a century, globally and continuously. They are stealing *the inheritance of the world's population* in a 'legal' way, because they have the 'co-operation' of local authorities, or governments who are ignoring their responsibility to treasure and preserve their priceless virgin forests.

During *this* new century, this climate-affecting felling of the rain-forests has actually *increased!* As a consequence, we are now watching the beginning of a violent climate-change leading in the direction of a world-wide disaster. As the characteristics of this climate-change become more and more visible it may finally become believable by everyone.

Little strokes fell great oaks: This whole cycle of cause and effect is already very visible and is simple to understand. Yet the world population does not protest massively against the destruction of the rain-forests, but nor do their governments. However, since the companies that effectively control the rain-forest destruction are multinationals, working in many different countries, they can only be *effectively* corrected by a multinational authority that *also* takes environment response ability. The 'United Nations' is the clear choice here but they are still not motivated enough to be prepared to control, or forbid this burning and felling."

The boy had been very quiet. He had listened carefully to the explanations and had appreciated the atmosphere of the presentation. It had been like listening to a neutral observer, a reporter, speaking calmly and without emotion, and delivering just the facts.

* * * * *

"But why is it, then, that politicians have spoken only about planting trees as a way to control the surplus carbon dioxide? Only as a way to try and compensate for the gases produced by burning fossil fuels? Why have these policy-makers never spoken about protecting the huge amount of rain-forest trees as water pumps which, free of charge, and without investment or maintenance costs, keep the humidity up to the mark and also help to maintain temperatures within limits? Something which protects the world's population from the disastrous consequences of climate extremes– of climate that is too cold or too hot; too dry or too wet and even cyclones?" he had asked in sincere surprise.

"Through lack of both insight and oversight" had been the prompt answer. This had been followed by the comment that those policy-makers had little insight and were ignorant of the law of cause and effect. Just as little insight as the people for whom, and on whose behalf, they made that policy. At best, those policy decisions were based on some cursory information that they had read about the issue, but almost never on their own knowledge or experience.

"Their information is based on knowledge from others, who in turn got it from others. Knowledge based on experience and perceptive observation is notably absent or, in the rare case that it is not so, it is discounted as irrelevant or 'not scientifically established'. In essence, the '*wisdom*' is missing. Also the realisation, the awareness, that knowledge, even scientific proven knowledge, is in fact only a resource for the process of gaining wisdom.

At a deeper level, the wisdom that everyone is bound to everyone else, and everybody with everything, is also lacking: as is the wisdom that all that is alive must be given proper respect and consideration, instead of being made subordinate to 'the rulers of creation'.

Also, when the persistent fantasy that human life can dispose of other lives, at will, becomes exposed, more 'value' can be given to other fauna and flora. But there is still a pernicious, (mainly 'Christian') fantasy which leads to the insane concept that the life of fellow men may be ended, unpunished, *provided that it happens on a very large scale*, and as long as those that have this right are suitably dressed, in camouflage green/brown, when they carry out their actions. This fantasy is generally politically motivated, although occasionally it can be rationalised that the motivation is 'noble' and therefore 'authorised'. That this concept could be legitimised, defendable, pardonable or even 'god-pleasing', for whatever reason, is incomprehensible – especially while the 'god-pleasing' solely concerns the *false god* of their own egos, and is used only to legitimise this false, *supposed* authority."

* * * * *

"Returning to the question of climate, it was explained that: "Climate has always fluctuated between warm and cold, with all the consequences which this means for life. The cycle of world climate, like all things in this dimension, has always existed as *pairs of opposites*.

Opposites which at a certain moment change into their opposite kind and can, at a certain moment, change into their reverse.

Climate is a complex mechanism which is not yet fully understood by anybody. Neither is the exact influence of trees, but it is clearly recognised that these have an important influence. They exercise such a complex influence that it cannot be overlooked and is just as difficult to manage as the increase in the use of fossil fuel – and the need to reduce the emissions of carbon dioxide.

The alternative for these fruitless efforts to stabilise the world's climate, and the world-wide state of the weather, is obvious. Through a positive and strenuous action to deliver a fruitful effort to improve and stabilise the psycho-social world climate.

With this approach, we go from confrontation to co-operation; from selfishness to 'selflessness'; to the acceptance of equality and the ability to establish equal world trade possibilities by ending protection of one's own interest through the power of money, at the cost of others.

And finally, voluntarily to equalise this power-powerless relationship and stepping back from thinking in terms of models and extrapolations and projections. More of the same doesn't create new possibilities and opportunities, even less by just planting more trees for the so-called damping down of more carbon dioxide discharge.

Changing of the psycho-social climate ourselves can be done by using our own sphere of influence. It concerns our inner world and on this we can *directly* exercise influence *ourselves*, contrary to the world climate in our outer world.

Planting or sowing more trees with great zeal will only lessen the carbon dioxide discharge if we preserve the still remaining rain-forests *and* introduce the 'hydrogen economy' on a large-scale. That mentality, and change of technology, will increase well-being and create new possibilities.

The introduction of a hydrogen economy, in this century, is unavoidable with the correct changes in society. History shows us how changes in society brought in the petroleum economy in the last century, which, in turn, followed on directly from a half-century of coal and steam economy. However, this new transition will be quite more complex.

In a hydrogen economy our solar energy, solar generated electricity, will no longer be wasted. The use of on-the-spot electrolysis of water (splitting the water directly into oxygen and hydrogen) is also highly effective. When the gases are re-combined, in the proportion of one to two, they form water again and release the energy that was used to split them in the first place. This 'stored power' is released again as solar energy. These gases are easy to transport from places where permanent sun makes electrolysis cheap and easy – as actually happens today now with barrels of oil and oil tankers.

The sooner we take advantage of the opportunities offered by a clean, durable economy based on the use hydrogen, the better. As soon as governments decide to stimulate and facilitate the necessary infrastructure for solar-gas fuel distribution, decision makers in the car industry will decide to further develop their already operational prototypes for hydrogen & electrically powered vehicles, and put them into large scale production.

Governmental action can end 'the chicken and the egg' paradox that holds back the use of hydrogen fuel in vehicles. The possible resistance of oil companies can easily be avoided by granting them a favourable tax regime and an interesting, but limited, time for investments in hydrogen production and distribution. They can also let go of the attempt to force them into bio-fuel diesel and instead provide the opportunity to make a profit as the new hydrogen energy carrier for an unlimited period of time. Bio-diesel's social and ecological side effects – and its limited replacement capacity – clearly disqualify it as a sustainable solution to the problem.

In the current situation, where the world's oil supply still leaves us time for a transition period, the change to a *real* solution can be phased in and the old methods phased out. A unique and precious period in which a selective and rational change can arise from the change from old to new energy systems. By postponing this transition period as long as possible it becomes shorter and more stressful, together with the increased chance of more serious conflict.

Also of importance in a fast transition, in the short term, is to be able to continue to use the oil which remains, but over a much longer period, and by more intelligent applications than primitive burning. The burning of fuel will also have to be reduced by severely restricting air travel – which in the first instance will certainly mean less frequent flying, and no more flying just for sun, fun and flowers."

"It sounds as though no real environmental problem exists unless you observe with interest the greenhouse effect but aren't impressed by it," he had said and then asked *how a start with such a hydrogen economy could be made?*

"To begin with the last point..." the man next to him has said while he slowly let himself slide down from his stone, and into the water. "When everyone becoming aware that there is an alternative to that scarce and expensive oil – with its catastrophic side effects on the climate – and that the alternative is within reach and that its introduction will have only short term sacrifices and discomfort... Then the hydrogen economy can begin.

This awareness starts with influencing people by setting up a communication plan containing information for all the different categories of users: like families, companies and governments. Information which will make it apparent that the introduction of a long-term plan will be profitable for everyone. Moreover, they need to know the details of the plan as well as the time period for introduction and priorities will have to be set and communicated.

Just as a short term space programme was started in order to land - with huge effort - a man to the moon, so a *long* term strategic energy programme must be started *now,* in order to prevent the necessity of 'sending' more than a billion people *for a walk* 'to the moon'. Which means: all of them going - involuntarily – straight to heaven, hell, or Allah.

For the rest, a country in which more than a quarter of the world's population lives, can, by taking the lead in this plan, become a leading force in the world economy in the second half of this century. Their structure of centralized power is an opportunity and an advantage for taking this kind of major decision.

As a result. it will provide itself with a solid, structural cost advantage, coupled with – and based on – a socio-psychological stability. With everyone's well-being as prosperity, instead of prosperity at the expense of everyone's well-being. It should no longer remain as it is today: barely paying the crowd for all their labour, and often in inhumane and abusive circumstances.

Of course, to establish a whole new kind of 'solar energy' industry in the southern European countries – such as Spain, Italy an Greece, where there is plenty of sun and space – is an interesting opportunity and should be an intelligent strategic decision for the European Union as well.

No, the environment does not have a problem; nor does the climate. This is not where the problem lies.

* * * * *

"Mankind has a problem:"

"For mankind, the problem is that seeing, hearing, feeling and tasting, stimulates *the desire to possess*. It does not understand that perishable things only are meant to practise with, not to identify with and be burdened by collecting them. By being blinded is not capable of recognising that greed is stimulated and cultivated instead of being minimised and marginalised. This happens because of our instinctive identification with the ego and a narrowing of consciousness. When this is the case, it becomes quite impossible to live from the soul.

This emotional and psychic pollution from one's own inner world results through living one's life to the full, in spoiled ground, water and air. As a result of this, physical health in such an outer world also deteriorates.

This narrowing of the consciousness results in, amongst other things; the neglect and persistently continuing denial of the profound effects of carbon dioxide discharge on both the flora & fauna of this world as well as on the inhabitants of low-lying islands and coastal areas whose life is at risk.

This asocial psychic inner-climate shows itself through an outer-weather climate which for the physical human becomes less friendly. Remember that both environment and climate can continue their existence, effortlessly, without any 'help' from mankind. Without problems!

It is time that mankind's *perception of itself*, and the outpouring of such inadequate behaviour, is *recognised, named and given priority* as the central problem – *'The mother of all problems'* – individually as well as collectively; actively as well as passively; without exception. As it is inside, so will it be outside!

The invisible brings forth all the visible. Also, consciously as well as unconsciously, the human performs the duty of past creations, co-creating: not just their offspring but also the circumstances before them.

Creating important surrounding conditions in favour of, or at the cost of, himself and of that offspring."

* * * * *

After this his father had remarked, while he lay down again to dry off, stretched out on his back, that he estimated the temperature of the water at 16 degrees.

On the warm stones here in middle of the river, life at once seemed to laugh at him:

What a game of hide and seek and passing of the buck.

How a life could be wasted, by acting in an interested way but without meaning, if he did *not* realise, within himself, his real capacity as a human and should let himself be sucked in by the prejudices of others who did not know what they were talking about; into the beliefs of professional chatterboxes, raconteurs of fairy tales who create for themselves an ego-flattering life without necessary effort for value adding work; or, into the hope that 'later on all will be become better' and profit making from those who – in the meantime – do all they can to maintain the status quo, and of course, their own positions, at the cost of others who are supposed to make careers by expending their best efforts.

What simplicity. What a relief. What a revelation. To be here already and to be connected. With himself, his father, his dead friend, Nature, his own nature and also his beginnings.(his origin)

To have to achieve nothing; or still want to do this.

To be the living proof of the universal, eternal and unchangeable life energy, in the time; the eternal Now. To have to prove nothing other than to have understood that. To live according to what the heart suggests.

* * * * *

Ignore all the so-called 'challenges' of one's ego and the egos of other people. Make confrontations with them impossible. Letting go all fears, based upon extrapolated fantasies by dissolving them in confrontation with the internal, ever-wakeful, observer. And with that, preventing one's own inner pollution and conflicts. What a simple life, what relief, relaxation, and perspective.

He inhaled deeply and felt very spacious inside. From now on he would not have to load himself up with information, from knowledge that isn't wisdom but about part of the reality which isn't reality. An illusion, because the true reality is indivisible. Not containable, discussable, transferable or predictable. Not to quantify, neither to reproduce.

The true reality is by living in the now, permanently, created for oneself, is thus created. In universal wisdom, when that happens consciously. Wisdom that goes beyond all comprehension.

* * * * *

He had let himself glide off his stone into the water to cool down and had asked himself:

How is it still possible that something other than the sun could be seen as creator of all life?

Reminding himself how he had been impressed during that story about a volcanic eruption that took place around a century and a half ago. Explosions which caused so much smoke and ash to arise that both sunlight and sun warmth were significantly obscured. And through that, all growth and life were severely diminished for several years. In making the universal, eternal and unchangeable life energy visible and palpable, the sun is still just one aspect in the universe. Just like myself, passed through his mind.

Why is it so difficult to understand that what *really* counts is elusive and inconceivable? It manifests itself equally both outside and inside myself; embracing everything and everyone; manifesting itself in everything and in everyone.

At that moment, his father's creed flashed across his mind. For the first time since the conversation in which the 'churches are tombstones' had resulted in an explanation which concluded with his own experience;

> *I am a part of the whole*
> *and the whole takes part in me.*
>
> *In every place in every time,*
> *at home in my eternity.*

* * * * *

He was moved, and felt that, in these days, this represented his own experience just as much as that of his father, even while there was nothing more said about it. He had very simply brought him here then let him experience and discover for himself.

In four quarters of a day I have learned more here than any university could have conveyed in four years, he thought thankfully. With a smile, he remembered how strange it had been in the first instance when he had heard that short conclusion.

Picturing to himself the concept of 'time'; past, present and future. By 'place', various countries; or if need be continents instead of the eternal Now, but here in the duality, forming part of the one universal dimension.

"At home, in my eternity" had risen completely above his comprehension and was therefore, experienced as somewhat theatrical. But still, the identification of the inner unchangeable, always-present, observer had been captured aptly in a few words. He understood that now, with a light feeling of awe; of awe and amazement.

* * * * *

In the water, the temperature was around 20 degrees lower than his body temperature and he had cooled down so much that he suddenly longed to feel the warm smooth stones against his chest and stomach. Sun warmth, sun energy. No longer the ever-growing vegetation the sun energy carries, but water. The now abundantly present water.

No longer the warmth of pressure from countless tons of earth, rocks and even many tens of metres of seawater as intermediary. But easy energy and able to be created through large areas of connected solar panels and electrical current.

To let the economy, based on the scarcity of energy, pass into one based upon an energy abundance with, as discharge residue, the same water. He had burst out laughing at the thought of the energy of the sun generating power stations in the hot areas with infertile soil. Or even near Mediterranean sea coasts, splitting salt water into gases which, after use in cars, would manifest themselves as small water jets or small steam clouds.

The idea that the waste product of an electricity power station in a not very sunny country could be drinking water...

And with that, making the deadly radioactive waste producing nuclear power stations, redundant. By this one development, finally turning them into museum pieces.

Many small safe power stations in dry areas. What a perspective. Not complicated. Easy to make, maintain and keep operational.

He woke up, startled by his father's voice which had suggested walking back to the car so that they could leave after lunch and sleep in their own beds again tomorrow night.

The request to leave this valley had felt so illogical. So unreal that he had been completely unable to react to it.

"You can depend upon it that the valley now forms part of yourself. You will notice that you will take the essence with you. That it will not stay behind and you never will lose it," his father had said.

Intuitively he knew it was true. Just as true as the fact that he would never lose his father. The man who now, *consciously,* formed part of himself, would never be able to leave him because of that. Could only leave him *behind.* Could only 'leave' him as his inheritance. Through carrying on ahead of him , by already living of his death.

Epilogue

"I don't "want to be a thing, or *just* a woman, but human, together with you," passed through his mind while he took hold of the baby boy from the nurse. In experiencing togetherness he had, at her request, given himself completely and through that perpetuating their being-human.

After the insight obtained in the valley of Tavascan, he had appeared to be capable of embracing her to his heart. He had, by his own accord, given her entrance to his life, this life of falling and getting up. During the voyage of discovery of his own interests and qualities, in relationship with his possibilities, over a pathless path of living day by day, doing what his heart suggested to him. Already years ago now.

Her; "Because I love you", she had turned into concrete behaviour, by accepting his refusal to promise her eternal fidelity. By being contented with his statement: "As long as we feel together, we will be able to live together."

He had explained to her how 'not to live in – or for a future, but in an eternal Now'. On which basis he was unable to form a contract like paying a monthly amount to the same bank for 30 long years. Neither to be able to make a serious promise for daily, or even weekly, to cherish the same kind of love and to express it to the same woman. "Why don't you look for a more suitable marriage candidate?" he had said to her, "if you would really like to get married."

"Because I love this young God. Because I want a man. Not an ageing boy," she had said with a laugh, without ever mentioning the subject again after that. And now she lay here, in their own second-hand on-site caravan. His girl friend from youth who had eventually found it time to become, with his help, a mother.

To now entrust him with the responsibility of fatherhood.

"He or she can go to school in the nearby village" she had explained. "At home our child will see how you earn your living by making electronic repairs in the extension."

It was true. His own boss; in the smaller on-site caravan which he had parked at right angles to the larger one. It was his workshop and also acted as a windbreak for the terrace. In this setup, over the past years, he had never wanted for work.

He easily could have been busy in it each day and earning even more money. Instead of spending Tuesday to Thursday in it with the other three days free to give his attention to writing and painting.

While she had added with a wink, "we shall call him Adam" he had thought back to his decision in the Tavascan valley:

To experience the paradise here, now. To be Adam.

About Hace

Hace was born during World War II, on 19 December 1943.

In April 1945 – during the battle for the liberation of the island of Texel – he survived an artillery bombardment on the village where he was born, but his father died in battle. Then, following this traumatic experience his mother never overcame the loss of her house, friends, neighbours and beloved and she withdrew from all human relationships.

Physically well taken care of, but emotionally disconnected from both parents at the age of only one and a half years old, Hace grew up and developed an autodidactic attitude in every aspect.

At the age of fourteen he studied the bible instead of schoolwork and made a conscious choice to become a Christian. At the age of sixteen he decided to join the Dutch protestant church and was officially initiated at the age of nineteen.

At the age of twenty two he was requested to become member of the church board of governors and served for six years. Three years later he was requested to take care of the spiritual education of the 14 to 18 year-old children of the church members. This he did, on a voluntary basis – two evenings a week – for ten years. During the first five years he worked alongside a protestant minister, and for the latter five years he worked with an ex-catholic priest. During this period he was also involved in the early stages of the Dutch movement: "Help rid the world of nuclear arms – and start by getting them out of the Netherlands".

Three years later, at the age of forty-five, he was asked to coordinate a protestant- church project to raise awareness about peace, justice and the environment in daily life.

In 1990 Hace co-founded an environmental foundation to give a voice to the local political minority and to protect the wetlands and long lake in his local area from the environmental abuse of chemical pollution and excessive building. He chaired the foundation for its first five years and is still a member of the board today.

In the autumn of 1990 he reached a stage of "total burn-out" and was effectively disabled by this for several years. During this period he reflected on the reasons why this had happened. Then, four years later, at the age of 50, taking all his conclusions into account, he re-designed his life. He divorced, after thirty years of marriage, and leaving friends, family, "certainties" and ambitions set out to travel for several years.

Following this he went into a one-day-a-week psychotherapy program for more than two years. At the same time he became a pupil of 'The international school of the golden rose cross', which he continued to attend for several years. During this period he also studied Gnostic writings, becoming aware the limitations of psychotherapy at the "personality level" and the necessity of focusing at "soul level". Also in this period, he became a working member of the oldest and purest Dutch naturists club "Sun and Life". He studied Tantra and annexed this form of Buddhism as a lifestyle. By doing so he re-socialised and re-educated himself into a natural, relaxed way of behaving and living and, as a consequence, also became a vegetarian.

He now coaches others to really enter into a crucial life change by encouraging them to develop self-confidence and personal growth, in order to —also— endure all stages of their transition.

At the age of 60 – when he had recovered from his life-long chronic depression and had learned to cope with his post traumatic stress syndrome, imposed memory and concentration restrictions – he left the Dutch protestant church, and left his country as well, to experience several months of solitude in the Catalan hills of Conca de Barbera. Here he was granted a state of enlightenment on the twenty-second of February 2004.

"*vader Zen zoon*" (father Zen son) was written during the summer of 2005 whilst staying in the Tavascan valley, in a small travel caravan, with his Catalan lady friend. During that period, Hace drew inspiration from being in his beloved Cataluña and being a naturist surrounded by nature in the vast Pyrenean mountains.

'**Ontology;** *the knowledge of being*', was written in the spring of 2007, in the unspoiled Pyrenean valley of Ager.

* * *

At seventeen, Hace left the parental home and went to England, where he was really not permitted to take on either paid or unpaid work. For several months he joined a team of road contractors, earning good money "by the yard". These adult weekly wages were mainly invested in profitable "merchandise" in later years.

At the age of twenty, when he had completed his two years of military service, he started doing shift-work in a steel factory and bought his first house. Then, at the age of twenty-one, five years after they first met, he married his school friend and eleven months later was presented with a daughter... who got a brother two years later.

By the time he was twenty-eight he was in a position to buy a larger house, with a study, and embarked on a three year marketing course. When he had finished this, and graduated, he started on his successful commercial career and became familiar with purchasing; sales; training; coaching; consultancy and management. This all resulted in leadership based upon authority through skills.

In the early eighties he was co-founder of a couple of companies but withdrew from them after the first year. He finally specialised in the generation of "new business": developing new product/market combinations and he operated as a consultant in strategic marketing. Throughout his life, he continued to combine paid work with unpaid volunteer work.

The environmental foundation was positioned as a new service/market combination through "non-profit marketing" and became effective through professional account management and structured communication.

After over half a century of survival, Hace now lives in both Spain and in the Netherlands. He enjoys living his life as a lover, writer, painter and nature photographer, and – every now and then – taking pleasure in flying his motorised para-glider alongside the birds of prey in the Pyrenees.

He is, at last, experiencing life-long happiness as a reality:

Always here & now, and never later/there.

Catalunya, March 2009.

About Ontology

U sually, we manage to completely overlook the fact that we are continuously making choices, and that when we make our choices they are based upon a judgment of available information. But how complete, or incomplete, is that information?

If our judgment about the information is coloured in any way, because a *pre-disposition* exists, then a correct decision will not be made, regardless of the completeness or reliability of the information.

In the same way, a clear judgment based on incomplete or unreliable information will not lead to a correct decision.

So how can we be sure about the quality of our information, and its source? Where do our predispositions come from? And how can we correct them?

Ontology focuses on *"the knowledge of being"*. This historical starting point, and the basis of all philosophy, has traditionally developed in two main directions; phenomenology and theology.

In this book, through a unique system of analysis and explanation, the synthesis of both has at last been made, and the philosophy of being, has finally been made accessible to all.

Anyone can use this new and uniquely suitable tool to reduce the stresses and fears that we encounter in everyday life (in particular those stresses caused by

unrecognized demagogy and our own pre-dispositions).
There is a good case to understand, and practice, this
philosophy of being. And if the time for that is taken,
it will lead to the development of a sustainable feeling
of freedom in a thoroughly satisfactory life.
For more information please check the website at
www.vaderzenzoon.com